Praise for W

"This book is an inspiring a
staying healthy and happy wh
to enjoy our lives – a... ɔu uu yuu."
The People's Book Prize

"A wealth of practical advice and information. This book is written from deep personal experience, including the steps you can take to recover from a really low point to reach a situation where you can regain your health and start to enjoy life again, without any feelings of guilt."
– Frances Leckie, *Independent Living*

"You highlight so many areas concerning care and wellbeing that are often forgotten, or rather, not dealt with."
– Andrew Richardson, CEO, *Friends Helping at Home*

"An uplifting and empathetic guide for carers, the book offers stories, tips and solutions to help make your life easier, safeguard your health and gives ways to enjoy life."
– *welldoing.org*

"Sara's book is brilliant. I am full of admiration for how she cared for her late husband and the way in which she is now helping others. Her energy, resilience and compassion are amazing. My partner is caring for her mum and she has borrowed the book and is finding it inspirational. I've also learnt from Sara how I can best support her and I hope the book is a huge success it deserves to be."
– Simon Fine, *Sixtyplusurfers*

"I found Sara's advice extremely helpful and her story is inspiring; she is very good at showing you how to look at difficult situations in a different way, so you can change your approach and become more resilient, healthier, and better able to care for your loved one."
– Member of the *Mobilise* Community

"There are other books on caring but this
is the best and a must read."
Robin Jowit, *Trustee of Countess of Derby Charity,
Kew and Patron of INS*

"It should be required reading for all carers. I just wish
I'd had a book like this book years ago."
– Irene, London, cared for her husband

" It has given me lots of invaluable information.
Thank you again. You have most definitely made me feel
better and given me permission to smile again."
– Jeanette, caring for a husband with brain tumours

"This book has provided me with insight and shown me
that I need to take breaks and start looking after myself,
something i have not been doing for many years.
Your book really opened up things for me that I had
been thinking but was afraid to voice. Now I feel that i have
been given the strength and confidence to take control back
of my life. Thank you so much, you have truly helped me
more than you will ever know."
– Claire, caring for her elderly mother

"I wish I had a book like this some years ago. It may have
changed some of my situations. My mum is in a care home
now, but I burnt out. This book is still a godsend for other
areas in my life though."
– Elizabeth, caring for her mother

"I've only just started reading your book, but I have been in
tears already. I have totally neglected myself and my needs
all these years. I am exhausted and tick every criteria of
Carers Burnout in your book. I'm making a promise to care
for myself and buying your book is my first step.
Thank you so much for all you are doing."
– Claire, caring for her son with a brain injury

Who Cares?

How to care for yourself whilst caring for a loved one

To my husband, Neal,
for his love and patience
whilst I found mine

Thank you to Rick and Bererley Mayston,
Peter Morrell, Piers Murray Hill, Lyun Frank,
Tatiana Kassessinoff PhD, Nadia Ghafoor and
Taryn Johnston for helping to get this book and
message out to all those caring for loved ones.

To my wonderful friends and family who have
supported me and Neal for so many years, and
finally, to my Mum and Dad – always there for us,
through the toughest of times. I love you so much.

Who Cares?

How to care for yourself whilst caring for a loved one

Sara Challice

FCM Publishing
UK

© Sara Challice 2024

This second edition published: 22nd August 2024 by FCM Publishing
www.fcmpublishing.co.uk All rights reserved.

The right of Sara Challice to be identified as the author of this Work
has been asserted by her in accordance with sections 77 and 78 of the
Copyright, Designs and Patents Act 1988. No part of this publication
may be reproduced, stored in retrieval system, copied in any form or
by any means, electronic, mechanical, photocopying, recording or
otherwise transmitted without written permission from the
publisher. You must not circulate this book in any format.

The information contained in this book is for educational
purposes only. It is the result of the study and experience of the
author. Whilst the information and advice offered are believed
to be true and accurate at the time of going to press, neither the
author nor the publisher can accept any legal responsibility or
liability for any errors or omissions that may have been made or
for any adverse effects which may occur as a result of following the
recommendations given herein. Always consult a qualified medical
practitioner if you have any concerns regarding your health.

British Library Cataloguing in Publication Data: A CIP record of
this book is available from the British Library.

Print ISBN 978-1-917377-01-0
Ebook ISBN 978-1-917377-02-7

Copyright of all illustrations and imagery used within remains solely
with their originator. No breach of copyright is implied or intended
and all material is believed to be used with permission. Should you
feel that your copyright has been impinged, please contact the
publisher to ensure appropriate acknowledgment may be made.

Cover and internal design by: Sara Challice

Contents

Contents

Short of time?

If you are a carer, with very little time to spare, you may not have the chance to sit down and read this book in its entirety, but you can dip into the various chapters as and when you need their advice, to help empower you and lead you to make better and healthier decisions.

About the author

Sara Challice is an award-winning author, motivational speaker and coach improving the lives of those caring for loved ones.

Having appeared on TV and radio, she regularly gives talks for local and national charities, and businesses supporting unpaid carers in the workplace.

After her husband fell ill will a brain tumour, Sara gave up her career as a graphic designer for a large investment company to care for him full-time. Following a stroke, he became bed-bound and needed full-time nursing care; due to the pressure, Sara became both mentally and physically unwell. She then found new strategies to regain her health and enjoy life again, even whilst caring for a terminally ill husband.

'Life is not about abstaining and enduring, it is still about enjoying your life, especially if you are a carer.'

www.whocares4carers.com

Introduction

As we all carry on with our busy lives, contemplating our hopes and dreams and making plans for the future, I don't think any of us would factor in the possibility of caring for a loved one during our lifetime. Why would we?

The truth is, any of us could find ourselves looking after a loved one. In fact, three in five of us will be in a caring role at some point during our lifetime. This may happen through a loved one falling ill, either mentally or physically, or becoming disabled or elderly. All we know is that they will need our help and support to cope with their daily life.

For many of us, caring is brief. We may help somebody on the road to recovery after they have left hospital, ensuring they have what they need to get back on their feet. Or else, we could be caring for longer, such as looking after an elderly parent who has become increasingly dependent on us, or bringing up a child with special needs. You may have found yourself caring for a loved one who has fallen long-term sick and is slowly deteriorating, meaning you may have had to give up work to care for them. Whichever situation you find yourself in, your caring role may take more and more of your valuable time and energy as you ensure another's welfare every day.

Every carer's role is unique, along with the person they care for. You could be offering a cup of tea and a chat to an elderly parent who would otherwise be isolated, or helping with their shopping and laundry. Maybe you are giving financial support and helping a loved one with form filling. Alternatively, a caring role could become more intensive, like washing and dressing a loved one, or turning them in bed to avoid pressure sores. However demanding your caring role is, all tasks take time and energy out of your own life.

If you are caring, you may feel that your world has been turned upside down and your life is not quite your own anymore. Life may have been hectic before, but now there is something more serious and demanding to deal with – a loved one's health, pushing your own wants and needs ever further backward. You not only have the daily stresses you had before, but you now have a new set of different challenges to cope with. Caring may feel harder than anything you have ever done before, but at the same time, it can also be the most rewarding and transformational encounter.

If you are stressed out from caring at the moment, this last line may jar. However, exhausting as caring can be, it can help deepen and strengthen a relationship, and enable you to develop skills you were not even aware of.

Every carer's role is unique, along with the person they care for

There are so many issues that arise whilst caring, many you wouldn't have considered when you first started out. Challenges can include healthcare; your relationship with the cared-for, your friends and family members; professional carers you hire and the emotional and physical difficulties you face.

Most of us are brought up with the idea that we should be there for others as well as for ourselves, but what if you are not there for yourself? What if you are giving all your time and energy to the cared-for and all those around you, but leaving yourself last? If you notice you are doing this, how long do you think you can keep going? Carers are remarkably good at juggling. Often, it's the only way to survive. Everything beyond yourself takes higher priority, seeming much more important, and it is easy to forget to be there for yourself. But there are only so many hours in the day and if we are so busy giving our all to others, there will be nothing left for ourselves. What if you are offering all your love and compassion to your loved ones, but neglecting to give love and compassion to yourself? This may seem a little bizarre. Why give yourself empathy? Surely the person you are caring for needs this at the moment, not you?

Being there for another, as well as for yourself, can be a difficult balance to get right

At the moment your health may be much better than that of the loved one you care for. Your cared-for may need your love and help right now, but if you continue to give emotional and physical support to another over a sustained period of time, this could eventually start to put stress and strain on your own mental and physical health.

Often, carers are so focused on looking after a loved one that their own wants and needs, including their health, are left aside – even to the point of cancelling their own hospital or doctors' appointments. They may simply not have time to attend to, or to leave, the cared-for. Therefore, being there for another, as well as yourself, can be a difficult balance to get right.

Even though caring roles differ greatly, there are many issues that arise for most carers. This book is designed to give you greater clarity and help you recognise who or what is, or is not, supporting you. It will also help you to become aware of how you are treating yourself. This is a big one. I disclose personal insights, which can help you recognise your own patterns of behaviour and ensure you have boundaries in place to keep yourself safe. Chapters including, 'Drop the mask', on page 31 and 'Taps and Drains, on page 131, will help to give you greater awareness and become more resilient around others. For more practical help, turn to, 'Making ends meet?' on page 111. Whatever your needs right now, there are many ideas throughout this book that could help you do something positive and constructive about your circumstances. Even if you are caring for someone who is very ill, there are still ways to ensure you safeguard your own health and happiness, so you can enjoy your own life once more. Believe me, sometimes the smallest of tweaks can make the biggest of differences. I, and other carers, have discovered this.

You are caring for two people – the person you care for and yourself

If you are in a caring role, did you know you are actually caring for two people? Not only your loved one, but also yourself. Many carers forget to be there for themselves because caring can be all consuming. But giving that same love and care to yourself is crucial if you want to remain well, not just for yourself, but for those around you.

Why do I say this? Because if you fall ill from the continued stress of caring, not only will you not be able to be there for your loved ones, but others will have to come to your aid. This is something a high proportion of long-term carers experience.

But when it comes to taking a vital break, many carers feel guilty taking time out to enjoy precious moments for themselves. Even when having a short break away from their caring responsibilities, their thoughts are on their loved one, instead of enjoying some well-earned rest.

It doesn't take long to become institutionalised as a carer – to become used to constantly giving to another. If you have been caring for some time, it could then feel strangely awkward to start focusing on yourself and your own wants and needs, but you still need to do this. Taking time to relax and do the things you enjoy will help you to recharge, so that you can remain happy and healthy, and continue to care for your loved one in a better state of mind.

You may be thinking that you don't have time to focus on yourself, or that you may be too tired by the end of the day to then think of things *you* want to do. Throughout this book, I share ideas and techniques to help make caring easier, which you can then use in your daily life. There's always room for improvement for all of us when it comes to managing our own lives, so we can enjoy the benefits. Tweaking different parts of your life will help you to find the time to breathe, think and act more clearly, so you are not run ragged by your constant responsibilities.

You may be a carer but you still deserve to enjoy life

We are all creatures of habit, so it is good to take a break and step back from our daily lives to gain greater clarity and become more aware of our situation. When we take time out from the doing, we can start to perceive how we are truly feeling and notice what we are doing every day – things we need to do and those which may be wasting our time and energy. In becoming aware, we are then able to make changes for the better and improve the quality of our lives.

I think you deserve to put your feet up for a few minutes and have a cup of tea. What do you say?

Our story

It's Saturday, 6 July 2013, and I'm in our little semi-detached cottage in Twickenham. The sun's up and golden rays are already streaming through the stained-glass windows in our kitchen. It's going to be another warm day, though I doubt I'll have time to venture outside to enjoy it. As I turn, I can smell the coffee percolating next to the kettle, sat on the old-fashioned red tiles. I need a cup to help wake me up as I didn't have much sleep last night. I feel dishevelled and it doesn't help that I've just thrown my clothes on this morning. I haven't had time to have a shower.

I feel a sudden urgency to check on him again. I hope he's okay. So, I dart through the dining room and into our small square living room with its yellow sofas. As my bare feet touch the soft beige carpet, I feel the peace in here. It's quiet and I can barely hear the clock ticking on the mantelpiece. I take a couple of steps over towards the small sash window with its net curtain and I peer over the cot side.

Ah, he's asleep and he looks so peaceful. I loved him from the moment I saw him. I check my watch. It's just another hour until his next feed. I suddenly give a huge yawn and become aware of how exhausted I feel. God, I feel so tired as I stare into space. It doesn't help having the baby monitor on every night.

Suddenly a knock at the front door jolts me and I go to

answer it. As I pull it open, I smile. It's Maggie. I love it when she comes over. We always have a good chat and a catch up. Maggie is nearly 60, with short grey wavy hair. She has kind eyes and is really down to earth. I always enjoy her company when she visits and we have a good laugh when we're together.

'Hey Maggie,' I call to her through the doorway, 'Come on in. How are you?'

'Yeah, good, thanks,' she replies. 'How are *you* doing, more importantly?'

'Oh, it's been a bit of a struggle. As with new mums not getting any sleep, I feel shattered.'

'I'm sure, love,' Maggie nods.

She looks thoughtfully at me and then smiles. 'Do tell me again how you met Neal. I love hearing about you two.'

I smile back at Maggie and recall the day I first met him.

'It was a special time and I remember it well. Picture the scene,' I say to Maggie, 'I have only been working in London for three days and I am on the 26th floor of the NatWest Tower. My desk is in a large, spacious office with huge windows overlooking great views of the city. I am part of the design team for a large corporate. *This* is where my life is really going to start.

'So, I am sitting at my desk, thumbing through the brand guidelines with the tapping of keyboards in the background. I look up and there he is. Neal. He's six foot four, the size and stature of a rugby player, and he is filling the doorframe. I am told he is our print supplier and, with a cheeky smile, is holding six bottles of wine for us all for Christmas. Neal looks over to me for the first time and says, "Good morning, Sara. I've got something here you might like." A man after my own heart.'

Maggie laughs as I continue.

'He often takes our design team out for lunch and so I get to know him really well. I always enjoy his company. A few months later, he asks me out and we start dating. We're having a great time. Neal is the perfect gentleman and he's got loads of mates – he's really popular. He's also captain of Hampstead Rugby Club and I go and watch him play.

'Then one day, not long after we've started going out, he turns to me and tells me he thinks I'm the one. I'm taken aback and I need a bit of convincing. But not long after, whilst Neal is driving us over Tower Bridge in his dark blue Mercedes, I happen to look across at him and surprise myself by saying that I could spend the rest of my life with him. Neal turns to me and replies, "Yes, and I could spend the rest of my life with you too." Little do we know what those words would later mean.'

Maggie and I look sombrely at one another.

'He begins having a few headaches and pins and needles down one side of his body. We are thinking it is just stress, although he's always so calm and we are enjoying life together. Then, one evening Neal is unable to get up off the sofa. I call an ambulance and he is kept in hospital overnight for observation. In the early hours, whilst he is asleep, I head home to get some rest. The following morning, the hospital calls me and asks me to come immediately. They have found something on the brain scan. Brain scan? I order a taxi and, during the journey, I feel tense and teary because I sense the news is not going to be good. I arrive on his ward and find him lying in bed with the curtains drawn around him. As I give Neal a big hug, a doctor at his bedside informs us of the dreadful news. Neal has been diagnosed with a large, malignant brain tumour. It is a shock for us all. He has been so fit and well up until now. Since then Maggie, if it wasn't for you and the other paid carers, I don't know what I would do.'

Maggie puts her hand on my shoulder. I continue, with tears in my eyes, shaking my head.

'This is not how it is supposed to be. After his diagnosis, Neal endures a long operation to remove most of the tumour, then six months of chemotherapy and six weeks of radiotherapy. We are at the hospital every week for months. He has another scan just before Christmas and we receive the wonderful news from his neurosurgeon that Neal is all clear. The tumour has gone! It is such a relief for us both. We can get on with the rest of our lives together. The following Christmas, Neal proposes to me. We see a great future together, but only three weeks later, his regular quarterly scan shows the tumour is back but this time it is inoperable. We can't believe it. Later that day, even though Neal sees me as the one, he turns to me and says that I don't have to marry him. In the blink of an eye, I turn to him and say, 'Stuff the cancer! We will make the most of what we have.'

Later that year we marry and see the day as a celebration of life with all our friends and family. It is a wonderful day.'

Maggie and I smile at each other. I look away as my smile dissolves and my voice changes.

'But it's been 11 years since then. Neal is now so poorly and disabled after years of chemotherapy and finally succumbing to a stroke. I can't bear him lying in that hospital bed in our living room, with the cot sides up. We can't even have a conversation, now that he can't speak due to the brain damage. That feeding tube in his tummy keeps getting infected and I always keep a close eye on him, just in case he has another choking fit. My wonderful, larger-than-life husband is reduced to little more than a body in a bed.'

I look beaten as Maggie gives me a big hug and I wipe away the tears. She heads off into the living room to wash and dress Neal. I compose myself whilst I pull the hoist from the back of the dining room and wheel it through towards Neal's bed. When he is ready, we can transfer him from the bed and into his wheelchair. Once he is up, I start to organise his medicines ready to administer into his feeding tube.

It's a tragedy for both of us. I do my best to deal with the situation, because when you love somebody, you do what's right for them, right?

Not only is Neal slowly losing his life, but I feel like I am losing mine. But you carry on regardless, don't you? What else *can* you do? Neal's physical health has now been in decline for years and he's becoming more and more difficult to manage. Also, not only do I have to deal with the continued emotional stress of not knowing how long he has left, but there is the physical side of moving and handling him. He's a big guy and I have already hurt my back a number of times whilst moving him.

The caring is relentless. Previously, I had no nursing skills but I certainly seem to have acquired some now. In the early days, Neal even called me Nurse Ratched, you know, from the film, *One Flew over the Cuckoo's Nest*? My caring role has changed considerably over the years. It is now nursing care, and it's every day and night. Even if I do get out, I can't switch off and relax. I feel like I am always on call. I also have to ensure a paid carer is with Neal if I am not, as he can't be left alone.

Though to help me through it all, I do love a glass of prosecco. Some nights it's a glass, others it's the bottle and some evenings, when I do get the chance to go out, I can drink my own bodyweight in fizz. When I do go out and see friends, I practically bounce off the walls. I feel like it's a get-out-of-jail-free card. A few months ago, at a family birthday party I was really letting my hair down, jumping around on the dance floor to the music like a four-year-old. My father's cousin asked him, 'What's your daughter on?'

And if you see me on Facebook, the only pictures you will find of me are with a drink in my hand, looking like I'm having a great time. Or should I call it Fakebook? You want to look like you're coping, right? Who wants to see me looking miserable and struggling? Anyway, it's Neal who's ill and needing help, not me, and, who wants to open *this* can of worms? So, I hold it all in and suppress my emotions for years whilst caring for a terminally ill husband.

The question is, how long can I keep this going? I haven't been feeling like myself for some time. Every morning when I wake, I have this gnawing dark feeling, like I have been at a funeral. I feel drained and depressed. Eventually the cracks start to appear. Due to the continued stress of caring, my immune system is suppressed and I fall ill with a nasty chest infection. It doesn't leave me for months and antibiotics are not touching it. Finally, I succumb to an MRSA infection in both ears. Now I am back and forth from the hospital, like Neal. We make a right pair! I am mentally and physically wrecked, whilst struggling to care.

One morning, my good friend Réagan kindly comes to look after Neal whilst I am at the hospital. She's a really close mate. Réagan is my age, 42, and South African. She has long auburn hair and a heart of gold. She's so kind and full of empathy. I feel relaxed in knowing I can leave her to care for Neal.

Later that day, as I arrive home, she greets me at the front door, but she looks annoyed, almost angry. In a shrill voice she barks, 'I hope you've got a pat of butter for your bottom!'

'Eh?'

'Because I'm gonna *slap* it. I had no idea what you do. I thought things were okay. You know, you're always smiling. Why have you been keeping this a secret?'

I look at her, perplexed. 'I haven't. I just get on with it. That's what you do. Anyway, I don't think anybody particularly wants to know. I get on with caring for Neal and get out when I can and make the most of it, but the following morning it's back to reality and I'm changing Neal's incontinence pads, dressing his pressure sores and wondering if this will be his last day.'

Réagan looks visibly shocked and she speaks in a low voice.

'You need help and not just the odd night out. You need more support and so does Neal. You can't keep going on like this. It's as if you're wearing a mask and pretending everything's all right. It's not all right. I've only been here looking after Neal for one day and I'm exhausted. You're running yourself ragged and I can see how tired you are. Can't you call family?'

I sigh. 'I have, but they're all busy. They have their own lives. Anyway, a few other carers and I have noticed that if you're the one to step up and care, other family members usually take a step back and leave you to it.'

Réagan looked deep in thought. 'You are not coping anymore. Who else can you call?'

'Ghostbusters?' I quip, despairingly.

'Nope.'

'Well, I could call Julia, the head nurse at our local hospice where Neal goes to the day centre each week. She's lovely and I chat to her frequently. I'll call her in the morning,'

The next day, I pick up the phone and call the hospice. As Julia answers, I begin to open up.

'Hi Julia, it's Sara. You know I've been ill for months now? Well I'm at the hospital each week trying to get myself right, but I just seem to be getting worse. I don't think I can cope anymore.'

There's a pause before Julia finally speaks.

'I've been expecting this call, Sara.' Her reply surprises me as she continues, 'You're one of our longest running carers at the day centre. Let me make some enquiries and see if we can get Neal in for emergency respite care.'

I sit back in my chair, relieved that I called her. I realise how dreadful I have been feeling. I have been doing too much for too long.

A few days later, I pack Neal's things into his brown leather holdall and sit on the edge of his bed in the living room. I explain to him that I will be away for only a few weeks and that he will be well looked after. I let him know how I need to rest and recover if I am to continue caring for him. I also assure him that I will be back to pick him up before he knows it.

Now, what to do during my break to get better? Staying at home alone in those four walls is *not* an option. I need to get away from it all and recover my health. I also recognise that a few hot stone massages aren't going to fix this. I need something deeper. I look online and find a meditation course beginning the following day at a silent retreat and manage to get a place. Silence. Just what I need, but would I be able to shut up for a week? The disclaimer on the website worries me. It states that a silent retreat may not be a good idea for people with depression. I know my mental health is not in good shape and I have been very low for months. Even so, I throw caution to the wind and book it. It's a basic retreat, so it's cheap, which is good.

Monday morning arrives and I drive Neal over to the nursing home and watch the staff buzz around him. I am relieved and know he will be in good hands. As I hug and kiss him goodbye on the forehead, he looks up at me wondering what's going on, even though I've explained to him what is happening. I feel the tears well as I walk away. I have done my best but I still feel like a failure. I don't want to leave him in there with strangers, but what choice do I have? We all have our limits and I have clearly reached mine. Looking back, the person I had really failed was myself. I hadn't been there for *me*.

As I climb into the car and put the key into the ignition, I sit for a few moments, contemplating all that has happened. I feel sad, but then I smile. I know this break away will do me the world of good and point me in the right direction.

As I take the long drive down to Devon, to the retreat, I think about all that has happened, now that I am away from the day-to-day chores and responsibilities. Over the years, I have felt quite isolated looking after Neal behind closed doors at home, although I am very good at putting on a brave face. I think about how I hurt my back moving him only a day after he had come home from the hospital. I hadn't been taught any moving and handling techniques. I had learnt the hard way, like most carers do, on my own.

Feelings of anger well up inside me. I have struggled with caring for a long time, but even so, there are certain friends and family members who have caused me grief, even judged me, although they can see I am caring for a severely disabled and terminally ill husband. I think back to the previous year when I put Neal into the local hospice so that I could have a desperately needed break. One family member had said in a very critical tone, 'I don't like him going in there.'

Well, neither did I. But what else could I do? At the time I needed the break. I had allowed this family member's judgement to make me feel guilty, as pleasing them seemed so much more important at the time. So, I didn't put Neal into the hospice again and I didn't get a break.

Funnily enough, this particular judgemental person didn't then say to me, 'Let me get my diary and see when I can come and help you.'

I had allowed others' criticism to be more important than my own health and happiness, and now I was too ill to care and had to leave Neal with strangers – something neither of us wanted.

*I had put everyone else first
and left myself last*

Over the next few days, I discover the silent retreat isn't easy. Whilst I stare out of the window of the former convent with my cup of herbal tea, I think of bolting for the car and driving off, but I know I need to stick it out and I'm glad that

I do, because a day or so later, light dawns and I gain clarity. I realise I have been suppressing my emotions for years, which has exacerbated my poor mental and physical health. I need to be more open and honest with others, and I also need to please myself and decide not only what is best for Neal when making decisions, but also what is best for me – for *both* of us.

By the end of the week I am feeling rested and better in myself. The silence has done me good; although I am not fully recovered, I am slowly getting there. It's going to take time...

A few months later I am back at home caring for Neal, but this time I am also caring for *myself*. I have regained my health and I am enjoying life again, ensuring I take time out to have regular breaks. I am also more honest with family and I ask for more help, which at times is offered reluctantly.

A few weeks later, I take Neal to our local charity quiz night. As I wheel him into the hall, a bald lady in her 60s comes running towards me. It looks like Carol, one of the other carers, but where is her *hair*? Like me, she has been caring for her husband, Jeff, for years. As I greet her, she exclaims, 'Sara, I bet you didn't recognise me. Did you know Jeff passed away a few months ago?'

I shake my head and give her a hug. She continues, 'And can you believe it? Only three days after his funeral, I was diagnosed with breast cancer.'

I am stunned as she tells me more, 'Not only that, but you know Gill, who cared for her husband with a brain tumour like Neal? Well he passed away last April and only eight weeks after he had gone, she was diagnosed with multiple sclerosis. She is already in a wheelchair and now her son is caring for her.'

'Oh, my word, Carol,' I exclaim, 'That's *awful*. You would think, after all you have both been through, caring all those years, now that it's over, you both deserve a break, but instead you are now dealing with your own illnesses.'

Later that night, I begin to wonder. These women are now coping with their own long-term conditions almost immediately after their caring roles have ended. I then ask them both if they think the continuous burden, and emotional and physical stress of caring, has finally impacted on their *own* health. Have they, like me, suppressed their emotions for years, ignoring how they are mentally and physically feeling? Sadly, they believe they have.

I then start to look into ways for carers to release their emotions, whilst managing their lives better, so that they can safeguard their own health, as I finally have. They are then more likely to remain fit and healthy to enjoy each day, whilst still being there for their loved ones.

I realise I have learnt so much over the years whilst caring, and I want to help others in a similar situation. As I talk to more carers, I help them to look after their health so they are able to actually start enjoying life again. We all deserve happiness, even during the challenging times.

We all deserve good health and wellbeing, especially whilst caring

Sadly, on 6 September 2015, my lovely husband, Neal, has another stroke and passes away. He is 55, and although I don't want him to go, I am relieved he is not suffering anymore. I have been caring for him for over 13 years.

I don't regret all these years of looking after him, but if I had my time again, I would certainly do some things very differently, and these appear in this book. I would then probably not have been so stressed, abstained from enjoying life or fallen ill.

Caring for a loved one can be so very difficult, but as I share my insight and stories, this information has already helped others in a similar situation. We owe it to ourselves to be healthy and happy. You owe it to *yourself* to be healthy and happy, even whilst caring for another.

So if you're caring for a loved one, it's time to start caring for yourself.

Neal and me on holiday in Gran Canaria,
July 2010

SECTION 1

It's all about YOU!

1

How are you?

Yes, how are you? Not the person you are caring for, but *you*. You may feel fine at present, but if you have been caring for a while, you may be a little frazzled around the edges. Whether you are juggling caring with work, or you are a full-time carer, you may at times feel worn down by the responsibility for another.

Often friends and family may ask how the person you care for is holding up, and it's great that they do. However, they can often overlook the carer who may be struggling to cope.

I look at it like this: even though Neal was the one who was ill with the brain tumour, I still awoke to brain cancer every day. It might not have been in my head but it certainly affected most areas of my life, to the point of leaving me completely drained. So, although you may not be the one who is ill, you may still be waking up to someone else's condition or illness daily and dealing with the consequences. Others will not realise this and often neither will you.

As carers are so busy focusing all their time and effort on a loved one, they often overlook how *they* are feeling and forget about their own health. Everyone needs love and care, and if you're caring for a loved one, you most certainly do.

The longer your caring role continues, the more difficult it can be to sustain your own health. Your own wants and needs are often on hold as you focus on another, and your social life may become drastically reduced. Your circle of friends may become smaller and you may feel you don't have time for yourself. In turn, your wellbeing may suffer, which may lead to poor mental and physical health.

Not only do a high proportion of carers forget to look after themselves, but they don't even think they are sufficiently important to merit any precious time or energy. I have heard a number of carers say, 'Oh, don't worry about me,' when I ask them if they are okay and getting enough support. They often feel there are so many other people needing help, with crucial matters to attend to, that they are not a priority. It's the nature of the role.

If you are caring for someone who is ill and who may possibly have limited time, you will be more inclined to give them of your best and put them first, leaving yourself last. If you feel this describes you, how long do you think you can keep living like this before you become ill yourself?

Are you giving too much?

In the United States, the term used for what happens to carers who give too much for too long is 'caregiver burnout'. Demands on a carer can become so great that they end up emotionally, mentally and physically exhausted. Symptoms can include:

- Feeling powerless
- Anxiety and depression
- Fatigue and feeling drained
- Feeling angry and resentful
- Having trouble sleeping
- Finding it difficult to concentrate
- Drinking, smoking or overeating
- Health problems.

I actually experienced one carer's 'burnout'. My neighbour, Nadia, has her own hairdressing salon next door and has a number of older clients. She rang me a in a panic: 'Sara, one of my clients has passed out!'

I threw on some shoes and jumped over the front wall to help. As I entered her salon, I saw a woman in her 80s slumped back in a hairdressing chair, hair in rollers, her eyes shut tight, white as a sheet.

Nadia started to explain, frantically. 'Pam has been caring for her husband for years. He is in his 90s and has mobility issues.'

I nodded and rested my hand on Pam's shoulder to let her know I was there. Nadia continued,

'This morning Pam was telling me she wants to take her husband to the doctor later, but he refuses because he does not want to discuss the lump he's found on his arm. They had an argument about it. She has been stressed all morning and, as I was talking to her, she passed out. Should we call an ambulance?'

I leaned over to Pam and checked her breathing and quietly asked her if she could hear us. With her eyes still closed, she mumbled she could. I asked her to breathe long deep breaths and to focus on that and nothing else. A few minutes later, she opened her eyes. She asked us to help her lie down on the floor, as she felt weak and nauseous. We made her comfortable on the floor with some cushions.

I was concerned she might have been having a heart attack, so I asked her if she had any pain or discomfort, but she said she didn't. She admitted this had happened before and believed it to be a panic attack. That provided some relief and I told her to continue focusing on her breathing and to have a sleep for 10 minutes to regain her strength.

Pam awoke a short while later, and as I sat on the floor beside her, she explained that she was stressed with caring for her husband. When she started to talk about the lump on her husband's arm, she immediately threw up. Her husband's health had literally worried her sick.

Still lying on the floor, Pam started to worry about others who needed to know what was happening to her. She asked us to cancel her husband's doctor's appointment later that morning, as she needed to go with him, and, at present, she clearly could not. She also spoke of someone named Laura, and asked us to call her.

'Laura will be angry when she finds out about this,' she fretted.

I was not sure who Laura was, but what I did notice was that, although Pam was too weak to stand up, not once did she think about herself. All the time she was worried about everyone else.

I found this astounding. As I continued sitting on the floor with her, holding her hand, Nadia called for an ambulance. Every time Pam started to talk about someone she was worried about, I put my hand on her shoulder and asked her to think only about herself right now. She was the one who needed help at that moment, more than anybody. How much further did she need to deteriorate before she finally realised that she needed to look after her own health?

A short while later, Nadia took the rollers out of Pam's hair and the ambulance arrived. The paramedics checked Pam over and helped her to the ambulance as Nadia and I waved her off. She was looking a bit better and I remarked to Pam that her hair looked nice. Well it did!

A few days later Pam was out of hospital and the following week she brought a bouquet of flowers around to Nadia and me, to say thank you for looking after her. I appreciated her kind gesture, but I told her she really shouldn't have and that we were very happy to help. Her health was the primary concern. She didn't want to have another panic attack and be left incapacitated.

Although I had spoken to Pam about the importance of looking after herself, I discovered later that year that she had died, leaving her husband without her love and care. This saddened me, as Pam was a lovely and kind-hearted woman and had been there for everyone else, but had not been there for herself.

Many carers place unreasonable demands on themselves and feel the responsibility for another's health is theirs alone. They feel they are never off duty, even if they do leave their loved one for a short break. Continued stress can build up bit by bit, and go unnoticed, as the carer becomes accustomed to the pressure. Finally, this can suppress their immune system. It isn't until their health becomes physically impacted that they realise they have reached their limits and cannot keep going as they have been.

Coping with caring can feel like treading water, though in reality you may be slowly sinking. Often, it isn't until we hit rock bottom and fall ill that realise we have to make changes to recoup and safeguard our own health.

The best solution is not to wait until a crisis strikes and to ensure we keep an eye on our own health, as difficult as this can be at times.

The pressure can build up,
bit by bit, and go unnoticed

Our family lived miles away and the burden of Neal's care fell on my shoulders. As he slowly deteriorated, I made myself solely responsible for his life – a difficult role to master considering he could be gone any day. It was constantly draining. During this time, I thought I was coping. It wasn't until years later that a volunteer at our local day centre, where Neal spent a few hours each week, remarked how I had looked just before I had fallen ill.

'You looked terrible,' he exclaimed.

'Thanks!' I retorted. 'So why didn't you tell me?'

'I didn't really know you back then,' he replied.

His observation surprised me. This guy, who had hardly known me, could see I hadn't been coping. How come *I* hadn't seen it coming? As mentioned in my story in the previous chapter, the result of neglecting my health ended in months of illness. Neal then had to spend time in a nursing home whilst I recovered, which was something neither of us had wanted.

How had I managed to ignore how I had been feeling for so long? And why do so many of us in a caring role neglect our own health?

Are you not important?

Think of a great movie you have watched, like *The Sound of Music*. In it, Julie Andrews plays Maria, a nun, who knocks on the door of the Von Trapp family. She has come to look after seven mischievous children after the death of their mother. In essence, she is a carer. Throughout the film, Maria brings much-needed love, kindness and a sense of fun to the family.

Now imagine the producers and editors have decided to axe Maria's part in the film. She has been taken out of script and out of the movie. The children have still lost their mother, but the pivotal character of Maria does not appear. Is this still going to be a good movie? Probably not. The children will still be missing their mother's love but they will not be nurtured and comforted by Maria, and there will most definitely be less singing and twirling around on a mountain top.

Now picture yourself as the starring role in the film of *your* life – and right now, you are. You are there for others, whilst caring for your loved one. You enjoy spending time with friends and family and strive to keep everything going.

Imagine – as with Maria – your script and your part have been cut from the movie of your life. There's a huge gaping hole where you used to be. Is this film going to be any good? What will happen to the loved one you are caring for? Won't your friends and family miss you? Not only that, but won't there be wonderful experiences that you will miss?

Maria was pivotal in *The Sound of Music* and you are most certainly pivotal in *your* life – *and* in others' lives.

Many carers feel they are unimportant, but *you are important*, not just for your own life, but to those around you. Self-love, self-respect and self-care are crucial, if you are to remain healthy while looking after a loved one.

We all need love and care and so do you

What can you do to avoid caregiver burnout?

Awareness is key

Carers can become so absorbed in their role that they forget to notice how they are feeling, both emotionally and physically. Have you even asked yourself lately how you are feeling? Just asking yourself this simple question can help you to gain clarity on how you are actually doing.

Have you laughed this week, or even enjoyed any of today? How is your physical health? You could give yourself a 'body scan' from the top of your head, down to the tips of your toes. Is there tightness in your back? Carers often suffer from a bad back due to holding tension in their shoulders and/or moving and handling their loved one. If this is you, why not have it checked out or try some simple supportive back exercises?

A good way to keep track of your health and how you are feeling, is to maintain a journal. I started to write one, after another carer suggested it. She discovered journaling was a great help. By writing down your inner thoughts, you can monitor yourself on a regular basis. You can ask yourself questions, such as what is draining you and what could you do about it? Some things are out of our control, but there will be ways of coping with these. Also, focus on the good stuff. Has anything positive happened today? And what do you have to be grateful for? Jotting this down can make you feel better as can taking the thoughts swirling around in your head out and down onto paper. It can often shed a light on your situation. That is why journaling can be a useful tool to help you through challenging times.

As a carer you are so busy, but you don't have to write down all your thoughts each day for this to take effect, unless you find doing so helpful. You could write your journal every few days, or whenever a particular problem arises. This can give you a better perspective on what is happening and lead to you making better decisions.

Open up to others

If friends and family enquire how you are doing, are you honest with them? Many of us are good at keeping a stiff upper lip, so that we appear to be coping. We don't want to look like a failure, right? And anyway, if we do open up, they may start asking more questions, so it's better to keep a lid on it. If this is the case, how much longer can you keep suppressing your thoughts and emotions before this finally leads to physical or mental problems?

I suppressed my thoughts for years before I finally disclosed how I was truly feeling during a carer's assessment. When I opened up, I found myself uncontrollably sobbing in front of a complete stranger. During those moments, I realised how ridiculous I felt, and every now and then I would burst out into manic laughter. God knows what he must have thought of me. I'm surprised he didn't send for the men in white coats.

After the assessment, I headed outside into the fresh air and stood in the car park holding a soggy bit of tissue from all the tears and realised how dreadful I had been feeling for quite some time. These dark emotions had crept up on me unnoticed. By opening up, even to a stranger, I felt instantly better and resolved to put things in place to improve my mood, like exercising and seeing more of my friends.

If you are having a difficult time caring, could you open up to others? We all need to be there for one another, especially during the difficult times. Being honest with loved ones can be the first step to obtaining more help and support.

Who could you speak to? Do you have good friends or family members you could confide in? Do you have a good relationship with your doctor? Just airing your inner thoughts can help you feel better. Suggestions can then arise as to how to improve your situation. I found that some carers I met through local charities often had a better understanding of what I was going through and they would recommend support they had received.

If you feel awkward opening up to people you know, why not call a local charity or your doctor and speak to them honestly about how you really feel? Ask if they offer counselling to help release pent-up emotions.

Lift your mood

Even though you are caring, don't accept consistent feelings of stress and sadness as normal. We can become so used to feeling anxious that it becomes our normal way of being. Even whilst caring, you still deserve peace and happiness.

Is there anything you could do right now to help you feel

better? Why not watch a comedy or chat to a good friend to alleviate negative feelings? Taking a bubble bath or listening to good music can bring us back on track and make us feel better as well.

Exercise

Not quite everybody's favourite suggestion, and if you are feeling drained and exhausted, the thought of physical exercise will undoubtedly sound appalling. But our bodies need movement and it can be a great way to relieve unwanted stress. Just walking outside and breathing deeply can help you feel physically and emotionally better. Other gentle ways to exercise include yoga and Tai chi. I used to go for a run to the park in the morning, whilst Neal was still asleep. It did me good being out and breathing fresh air. I would watch the dogs in the park enjoying their exercise and this would put a smile on my face. I'd sometimes stop running and just walk. Outdoor space helped me deal with my inside space.

Getting into the outdoor space helped me deal with my inside space

Also, carers can become so pent-up and frustrated with their situation that this can lead to anger or aggression. Exercise can be a good way to physically release this. Trying out a kickboxing class or using the punch bag at the local gym could help. Or else you could try punching a pillow to release the tension.

Human beings are wired to seek pleasure and you may not be inspired to exercise, so instead, what's your favourite song to dance to? Why not turn the volume up and dance in the kitchen or your living room? This may sound a bit bizarre, but sometimes I do this to shake out the stress from my body. We often hold a lot of tension in our shoulders. If you notice tension in *your* body, try shaking it out to a good piece of music that lifts your mood. Dance like no-one's watching. Let's just hope the neighbours aren't looking over the fence.

Deep breathing

Most of us breathe shallowly due to poor posture, but deep breathing can release tension. Try lying down or sitting with your back straight. Fill your lungs slowly up from the bottom, starting with your stomach, then your chest and up into your head. Fill yourself right up and then slowly release the air in a long outward breath. Try this for five minutes and see how you feel afterwards.

Scream

If you are feeling angry or frustrated from caring, let these emotions out with a good scream. It is a great way to release suppressed emotions. I know other carers who have a scream once in a while. I certainly have. If you don't want to worry anybody who may hear you, you could scream into a pillow.

Cry

A good sob can release negative emotions. Crying is a healthy thing to do, whatever your gender. Many of us hold it all in, but if you are feeling sad, let it out. Crying can release stress and anxiety.

Check in with a friend or family member

A great way to take stock of how you are feeling is to chat with someone you trust on a regular basis. On Sunday evenings when I was caring, I used to chat over a cup of tea with my good friend and neighbour, Nadia. We were both carers and would ask each other how we were feeling and what our week had been like. We would open up and share our feelings. If any issues had arisen, we would make suggestions to one another about how to manage them.

Remember, there's only so much you can do for your loved one. You may not be in control of their health, or their thoughts, and you cannot control all outcomes. You can only do your best. You also need to do what's best for you.

So, taking regular stock with yourself or with a friend can be a good way of discovering whether you need more support or to make changes in order to improve your wellbeing.

Over to you...

You could try taking some time out to sit by yourself and jot down your inner thoughts on a pad or in a journal. This can help bring about greater clarity with your present situation.

If you can, jot down any ideas that come to mind as you read the following:

- Sit for a few moments, take some deep breaths:
  - o How are you feeling emotionally? What feelings are coming up? Are you feeling happy or sad, frustrated or calm? If negative emotions are coming up, why is this? Try speaking honestly to others to help you become more aware of what is not working and who is causing you difficulties.
  - o How are you feeling mentally (in your brain/mind)?
  - o How are you feeling physically? Do you have any aches or pains in your body?

- If you feel you need help or support with any of the above, please do not hesitate to contact your doctor, other healthcare specialists or charities. Just asking for help can set a positive ball rolling to help alleviate tension and improve mental and physical health.

- Who or what lifts your mood? Write a list of good friends or family members you enjoy being with. What things do you enjoy doing that help you to relax and make you smile? When you feel low you could call someone from the list of friends and family or choose an activity you enjoy doing.

- What sort of exercise do you enjoy doing? Do you like physical exercise like aerobics or something more relaxing, such as yoga? Are there any group classes you can join? Is there somewhere you enjoy walking? Maybe you can add a particular exercise to your daily routine, even for a short while.

- What are your favourite pieces of music? Why not make a play list to relax or dance to?

2

Number One

For a few moments, I would like you to think of everyone in your life – all of your friends and family members, those who live near and those who live a distance away. Out of all of these, think of those closest to you who really matter. For argument's sake, just choose one who is number one in your life. Who is top of your list? If you are married, you would possibly think of your spouse/partner? Maybe you would think of your mother or father, or a best friend you have known for years? For most of us, the last person we would think of is *ourselves*. Did you even think of yourself whilst doing this?

Guess what? *You* are number one in *your* life. If you are caring for someone who is seriously ill, your thoughts and feelings may be currently with them. But even so, the most important person in your life is *still* you. Carers often put those they care for first and themselves last. By constantly focusing all your attention on a loved one, it can become second nature to put others first. I have interviewed a number of carers and, even though I ask questions about *them* and *their* lives, they very quickly head straight back to their number one subject – their cared-for. It doesn't seem to matter how many times I steer the conversation back to the carer to see how they are, it doesn't take long before they return to their cared-for. We carers just can't help ourselves.

If you are caring for someone who is seriously ill, it is understandable that they need your love and support right now, but you still need to strike a balance to ensure you look after your *own* health and wellbeing.

At present, you may feel you just don't have the time to think about yourself. There will probably be a mass of doctors' appointments, chasing social services and financial issues to contend with, along with a host of other things to address. So it will be easy to bypass yourself and neglect your needs. You can deal with that later, when you have time – which never comes. Pushing back on your own wants and needs can lead to poor health if neglected, isolation due to not giving time to nurture other relationships, and even anger and frustration because you are not taking time to have regular breaks. If you leave yourself depleted and stressed, your cared-for will most probably sense this. Many find the responsibility of caring a burden, and it can quickly take over their lives. When this goes unchecked, they can feel they are purely existing for another – not a healthy way to live.

It's the nature of the role, constantly being there for another until you are not there for yourself

I know of a carer who needs a heart operation but refuses to have it, as he is worried about leaving his very disabled wife for whom he cares. It's understandable why he doesn't want to leave his vulnerable wife with others, but the alternative of not having the operation is an even bigger concern. Sometimes we just don't have a choice, because we need to ensure our own health and wellbeing.

We often have so much to juggle, trying to keep all the balls in the air, that we can end up exhausted and not in a good state of mind.

In the early days of caring, I would rush around, trying to do everything, and attempting to please everybody. This didn't do me any good. Looking back, I needed to slow down and say 'No' to a few things. It would have been better to leave space between each chore, instead of rushing to finish one before starting the next. Each day was filled with ticking off lists.

So, ask yourself: what do you really *have* to do right now? And does it need to be done so quickly? We can easily put pressure on ourselves. Do the cushions on the sofas need to be plumped up all the time? Does the house need to be spotless? What is more important, having a spotless kitchen and saying 'Yes' to everybody, or taking time to relax and ensure your mental and physical health are in good shape? I'm aware some of us will say both!

Find space in every day to focus on yourself. This may mean pushing back on what others expect you to do. Not everyone will be understanding. Sometimes friends, family and co-workers may not realise they are burdening you. They may presume you are coping and that you really don't mind. Communication is key to making sure they recognise you can only do so much.

When you make decisions, you need to ensure that your opinion is taken into account. Your feelings and your health are just as important as anyone else's.

Over to you...

- If you have moments in your day when you have time out, what do you usually find yourself doing?

- Are you doing unnecessary chores? Instead, can you leave these for a short while and focus on relaxing and enjoying yourself?

- Where can you push back and say 'No'? Being diplomatic with others, and making them aware you need time to rest and recoup, will help keep you healthier and happier.

3

Be kind to yourself

Carers are often known for their love and kindness, whilst selflessly putting others before themselves. Did you know that practising kindness daily can have great benefits for your *own* health, as long as you are not depleting yourself? So, not only is it good for the person receiving the kindness, but it can also be good for the one who gives. It can improve your mood, boost your serotonin (happy hormone) levels and lower stress.

Being kind to someone else can make you feel happier. I think of times when I would care for Neal and hoist him into bed. On winter afternoons, I used to put a heated cushion behind his neck and under his feet. He looked comfortable and snug as he fell asleep. The knowledge that he was safe and relaxed, even though he was very poorly, gave me a deep sense of peace. My time and energy had been well used. Making him feel better, made me feel better.

Have you noticed how you feel when you have done something for your loved one? Knowing they are cared for and safe can give you a sense of contentment. You are improving the quality of another's life. Psychologists call this 'helper's high'. Loving and giving produces endorphins, the feel-good chemicals in the brain. Being generous to others can help you to feel more joyful.

Also, by displaying kindness, not only do you and your loved one benefit from your act of love, but it creates a ripple effect around you. Others experiencing your generous nature may themselves experience an improved mood, inspiring them, in turn, to be kinder to those around them. Kindness can spread, which is great for our communities.

Not only this, but being kind has been shown to cause the brain to produce the hormone oxytocin. Research has shown that oxytocin reduces inflammation in the cardiovascular system. So, being kind to others can improve our own health, not only psychologically, but physically too.

> *'It is in the giving that we receive.'*
>
> St Francis of Assisi

Carers usually have a lot of kindness for others, though wanting to help everyone but yourself can lead to you neglecting your own health, and leave you drained. There needs to be a balance.

Caring for yourself

We are often told we should treat others as we treat ourselves, but what if you are not treating yourself very well? Do you sometimes criticise yourself or put yourself down? Caring can be challenging, but if you're also undermining yourself and treating yourself badly, you then have another layer of stress and unkindness to cope with. Often, it is when carers fall ill and are unable to manage that they come to realise they need to go easy on themselves, especially if they want to continue caring for their loved one. So be kind to yourself, both mentally and physically. You can only do so much. We all have our limits and you will have yours.

Practising self-compassion

Compassion means to 'suffer with'. Practising self-compassion is to give *ourselves* the same kindness and care we give to another. Carers may feel and understand the suffering of others, but often do not notice the suffering they too are experiencing. This mental and physical stress can sneak up on a carer, and after a while start to feel normal.

So, as your heart goes out to others who are suffering, allow your heart to go out to you too. If you are struggling to cope, try not to ignore this by putting on a brave face, but give yourself love and understanding. All carers have a difficult time now and then. Ask yourself how you can care for and comfort yourself to see you through.

Most of us have a critical and judgemental inner voice that picks on our shortcomings. We can be very good at beating ourselves up. At times I was quite horrible to myself. I was caring for a terminally ill husband and on top of that I was harshly criticising everything I did. This certainly didn't make for a pleasant day. Not only was I not there for me, I would put extra pressure on myself. I didn't think I had time to be there for me. It pushed me over the edge. No wonder I ended up falling ill.

If you treat yourself like a walking doormat, others will do the same

You are only human and you can only do so much for others. Many carers come up against themselves, judging and resisting, whilst getting increasingly frustrated. If this happens, the cared-for may notice your internal hostility and it won't make for a great day for them either. They may quietly worry or feel more of a burden.

Have you judged yourself harshly, even though you know

you are going through a difficult time? Are you trying to be too many things to too many people? By spreading yourself thinly, you aren't giving your best to anyone, especially yourself. You only have so much energy. We are all human and so are you, so go easy on yourself.

Your inner dialogue

It is good to keep a check on your thoughts. Have most of your thoughts been positive or negative? Carers can have so many worries that added negative thoughts can make them buckle under the pressure. Most of us worry about things that may never happen. What a waste of time and energy! For carers, that is energy they do not have to waste.

We all have chatter going through our heads every single day. Have you noticed what your usual inner dialogue is saying to you? Does it have a particular voice? Are there any catch-phrases that keep coming up? Most of our inner chatter is on a loop and recurs nearly every day. What is your inner dialogue saying to you and how is it making you feel? Is it critical or judgemental? Does it make you feel good or is it putting you down?

Be kind to yourself. It's hard to be happy with someone being mean to you all the time

When I was caring, I noticed I would take to heart any unkind or judgemental comments others had said to me and I would keep repeating them in my head, making myself feel even worse than I already did. Isn't it funny that if you are given five compliments in one day and one negative, the unpleasant comment is the one you focus on. That's exactly how it was for me. These judgements would swirl around in my head for days, or weeks, or even months.

How are _you_ treating you?

We can choose our thoughts, but we usually think the same ones. Our thoughts can then fall into a groove, such as worrying about a loved one, and then having recurring feelings of powerlessness and unworthiness. These continuous negative thoughts can eventually impact the body and make us ill.

If you notice many of your thoughts are quite dark, find a way of breaking that cycle. For example, think of happier times or something that previously made you laugh. This will not only shift negative thought patterns, but help to keep you happier and healthier.

We are taught to be there for others, but we also need to be there for ourselves

I know it might sound a little bizarre, but have you ever given yourself a hug? We can be very good at giving others love and attention, but how about turning that love and attention towards yourself? Hugging has great health benefits. If you hug another, not only can you give them and yourself instant comfort, but it can also cause a surge of dopamine and oxytocin (known as the love hormone) for you both, which helps to reduce depression and anxiety. Also, hugging helps to release tension in the body, by reducing the level of the stress hormone, cortisol. Whilst hugging, serotonin, the neurotransmitter responsible for your mood, also increases, making you feel better. So, hugging can help in a number of ways, by releasing good hormones into your body, reducing tension and making you feel calmer and safer.

Being kind to your body

As well as monitoring your mental state, it is good to check on your physical state. A high proportion of carers suffer from physical stress, so finding ways to reduce stress levels can prove very useful. Here are some tips that may help:

- Reduce alcohol intake and smoking. Both can increase the physical effects of stress.
- Try drinking less coffee or tea, as caffeine increases the stress hormones in your body. If you have four cups of coffee a day, try having only three. See if you feel better.
- Take regular physical exercise. It releases endorphins into the body, which can make you feel better. It doesn't need to be a full-on workout. Just going for a walk can relax your mind and body. While I walk, I sometimes listen to podcasts about health and wellbeing or to music. What would you listen to on your walk?
- When feeling pressured, push back and ask for help more often.
- Take regular breaks from caring, if you can. Just taking time out for 10 minutes several times a day to focus on yourself will help you feel better.
- Try to have enough sleep. Carers have many worries.Try taking your mind off things with a good book, just before you turn out the lights.
- Eat well. When we become stressed, we often reach for junk food or sugary snacks. Try cutting down on sugar, as this can often leave you feeling more tired afterwards.
- Look into local classes that offer relaxation techniques, like yoga or meditation. You can then practise these at home. A few simple yoga stretches each morning can relieve tension in your back. Ask your carers' centre if they offer any relaxation classes.
- Reach out and talk to others. You may have heard the

saying, 'A problem shared is a problem halved'. I found comfort in speaking to other carers going through similar situations, as not only were they more understanding, but they could also offer advice from their own experience. Local carer centres arrange meet-ups for carers.

> *'You, yourself, as much as anybody in the*
> *entire universe, deserve your love and affection.'*
> Bhudda

Give yourself permission

Many of us feel we need permission to do something good for ourselves. Why is this? Well, we may feel like we don't deserve it, or feel guilty about doing something kind for ourselves when our loved one is unwell at home. If they are not enjoying life, we may feel awkward in enjoying ours. At times, I certainly felt guilty about leaving Neal at home with carers to head out to meet friends and enjoy myself. What about *his* enjoyment? I knew he would be waiting at home for me and I would think how he was unable to enjoy and do the things we used to do together. His disablement was hard for both of us. As a result of this, in the early years of caring, I stayed in rather than taking a break. By the end of the week, I'd feel flat and not myself. I hadn't had any quality time for me. I was pretty much existing for another. By abstaining from experiencing any enjoyment, I became low. It's important to have quality time out and to find time to enjoy life. It does you, and those around you, good.

Turn your love inward

It's not good to give all of yourself away to another so that there's nothing left for you. With this in mind, if you were to give yourself permission to do one thing for yourself today, what would it be? What treat would you give yourself? Would it be a slice of cake, a massage, or if it were possible, a night out with a friend? Even whilst caring, you still deserve to have pleasures in life. So, try treating yourself, if you can, on a regular basis.

Over to you...

- Are you being *too* altruistic in wanting to be there for everyone around you but forgetting about yourself? Are there people or areas in your life where you can rein this in, so that you will then have time to yourself to be kind to you?

- Do you have any recurring thoughts? Are you worrying about something that isn't really that important? We often imagine worst-case scenarios – which in the end never happen – wasting our precious time and energy.

- If your inner dialogue is critical or judgemental, can you try changing this inner voice to have more love and understanding? Think of someone close to you who has your best interests at heart. Now imagine what they would be saying to you as your inner voice.

- If you are finding it difficult to give to yourself or feel you don't have the time, try making an agreement with yourself to do just one thing each day for you. It could be the smallest thing – like making a cup of tea and sitting down with a book for 10 minutes. Whatever you do that day, you could jot it down in a 'Being Kind to Myself' diary. Just put the date and what you did each day. This simple and quick act will help you to become aware and form a new and healthy habit of giving to yourself. This could start a positive trend to empower you to do more for yourself on a regular basis. Notice how you feel after just a few days of doing this.

- When we are having an off-day, we can feel low or stressed, and in doing so, we can't think clearly. So before another off-day strikes, you could make a list of the kind words others have said about you or compliments paid. Reading this will remind you of how positive you are in others' lives.

- Alternatively, create a box of things that make you feel better, like great past memories, photos of fun times or positive activities which make you feel good. If there's chocolate in there, the box could say on it: 'Open in case of emergencies!'

4

Drop the mask

Many of us are not honest with others about our true feelings. It's almost as though we wear a mask. We've all done it. We show others, like friends and family, a particular side of ourselves when, really, deep down, we are feeling very different. Also, we may show our best side to a doctor or other healthcare professional rather than opening up with what we are really thinking.

Why do we hide our feelings?

Many of us tell others what they want to hear because we don't want to upset them. Also, we may want to stay on their best side. Or else, we may put up a front because we fear being judged, don't want to look like we're failing or don't want to disappoint those around us. We prefer to look as though we are coping even if, in the end, this means falling ill from the stress, rather than being honest and telling it like it really is.

None of us wants to appear vulnerable or inadequate. Furthermore, we are not usually keen on telling someone how they make us feel if those feelings are negative. We would rather appease them. I think most of us prefer to complain to others, rather than to the person who may have upset us; rarely do we give honest feedback to the person who really needs to hear it.

It's about saving face – appearing as though all is fine, when deep down it isn't.

The consequences of people-pleasing

Many of us genuinely like to please others, but we may also people-please because we want to fit into society. We want to be liked. It's a coping mechanism, but it can have serious consequences when dealing with a difficult challenge like caring.

Have courage!

I kept my feelings under wraps with a particular family member for fear of being judged or in case we fell out. I didn't want this to happen, on top of the stress of caring. This family member was quite critical about me, even at times to the paid carers when I wasn't around. They didn't visit often but they could see I was caring for a terminally ill husband. Their flippant and often unkind comments swirled around in my head for months. I was struggling to cope and I felt they were undermining me. I wanted to tell them how they made me feel, and that I needed their support, not their judgement, but I loathed conflict. So when I saw them, it was as though I wore a mask. I was always polite, even though at times they had been unkind to me. I harboured deep resentment and it reduced me to tears. Have you ever experienced anything similar? I remember even crying on my disabled husband's shoulder one evening as he could do nothing but look on and stroke my back with his one good hand. Hiding behind my mask had serious ramifications because I suppressed these negative feelings for this person for years, and I believe this contributed to my eventual illness.

Continual negative thoughts brought about by another's poor behaviour, as well as caring, can push you over the edge. Even when unwell, many carers continue to wear a mask as they want to look as though they are coping and don't want to cause any issues.

For me, it wasn't until this particular family member did something so awful that I refused to turn away from their unpleasant behaviour any longer. I dropped the mask and spoke to them directly and truthfully for the first time in 10 years. It wasn't a comfortable conversation but things needed to be said. Bottling it up wasn't an option. During this phone conversation, my comments were respectfully noted, but I know this other person was not truly honest during the phone conversation. Even if you are open with others, they may not drop *their* mask. A leopard never changes its spots, but this family member did slightly improve after the conversation.

It cost me a lot to wear a mask. I had wasted so much time and energy over those years, fretting and stressing about how to deal with this person's lack of compassion.

We all have 'friends' and family members who push our buttons and cause us grief. It is the way of the world. The question is, how to deal with it? Caring is difficult enough, but suppressing our emotions can add further mental and physical stress to our body and to our health.

Being authentic

What does it mean to be authentic? It means to be who we truly are – without the mask. To be honest and open with ourselves, and with those around us, whatever the outcome. In doing so, we can then live a more liberated life, but it does take courage to let others know our deeper feelings.

When do you feel you are at your most authentic? I feel I am the real me when I'm enjoying the company of my close friends. We speak openly about everything, not fearing reprisals, and it is enjoyable and liberating.

Also, when do you notice you are not being true to yourself? From whom do you hide your real feelings? There may be particular relationships in which you feel you cannot be your true self. I have found this can often happen in the company of opinionated and judgemental people. They can reduce our ability to be our real selves. I find, whilst in the company of these kinds of people, I shrink and make myself small, so that those who criticise me see less of the real me. The unkindness of others pushes me away.

Set your boundaries

Sometimes, someone says something that oversteps your boundaries. They come out with a flippant comment that undermines the importance of all you do. It can be difficult not to take this personally. I have had family and healthcare professionals make remarks, not meaning to offend me I am sure, but all the same they have done so. My impression was that they just didn't understand the situation and what I was dealing with.

One carer, who has looked after her husband for nearly 30 years whilst bringing up their children, has often felt this. Every now and then, one of her sons comes out with a flippant remark that really hurts her. She has cared for such a long time and has done so very well, but such comments have undermined everything she does. She believes her son doesn't realise the impact of his words and how it affects her. I have suggested she pick him up on his negative remarks as and when they arise. Just making someone aware of the impact of what they say could at least make them think twice before they criticise again.

Know who you really are

We are all brought up to behave in a certain way, so that we integrate with society. From the beginning, parents, relatives and peers tell us what conduct they consider acceptable and unacceptable. Their own parents and peers would have given them similar guidance. By the time we reach adulthood, many of us are 'running on a programme', behaving in a way that fits in with those around us, instead of being our true selves and enjoying a life of freedom. So to fit in, we wear a mask and appease others, and are restrained by fear of reprisal.

When wearing the mask, which coping mechanism do you use?

We all have particular styles of communication that help us to cope when interacting with others. These can generally fall into four types:

Blamer	**Computer**
Pleaser	**Distractor**

Becoming aware of these four styles of behaviour (explained below) can help improve your communication with others around you. You may notice which archetype you fall under, as well as becoming aware of which of these best describes your family members. This can then help you to understand why some of those around you behave differently, or even at times create rifts or conflict. The four archetypes are as follows:

Blamer – Under duress, this person wants to dominate and ensure they exert their power. They may often be quick to blame others and tell them what they have done wrong. It doesn't matter whether the blamer is right or wrong, the main thing is to exert power. Blamers loathe surprises, wanting to know everything in advance, so they can stamp it with their approval. They can often be controlling of others, and situations. They also find it very hard to trust. Blamers can hide feelings of loneliness behind a tough exterior. At their extreme they may even seek to control others with guilt, anger or manipulation. They may have difficulty letting go of things, as their greatest fear is of loss.

Computer – These people can often appear aloof, or even cold, as they hide their feelings and show a lack of emotion. Although they may be bubbling like a pressure cooker on the inside, they can appear calm and cool on the outside. Computers may use knowledge as a weapon to avoid giving love or compassion. They may want to appear perfect and their biggest fear is being in the wrong.

Pleaser – People that fit this archetype want to rescue and help others. They also look for others' validation. Pleasers can often appear subservient and will usually accept any criticism as they deem themselves of less worth than others. 'Oh, don't worry about me,' you may hear them say. Pleasers seek approval and avoid conflict. Their main concern is how others perceive them. They need connection and they fear loss or rejection.

Distractor – People that fit this archetype are addicted to change and don't like to be hemmed in with making a commitment or a decision. Instead of taking positive action, Distractors will use a range of emotions to divert and avoid an issue. When others start to discuss a problem, the Distractor may ask, 'What problem?' and change the conversation.

When reading the four archetypes, do any stand out as a coping mechanism for yourself? Which do you feel best describes you? I believe my type, and that of many carers I know, is the Pleaser. I want to rescue others and make them happy even if, at times, it costs me my own happiness or I become stressed or ill in the course of it. You may notice that you are more than one of these types. You could be a couple.

You could also try noticing which of these archetypes your family members fit into. You may realise why you come into conflict with one person more than the others. In recognising their shadow self when dealing with pressures, you can then get a better understanding as to why they behave in the way that they do. We are all different, and this makes life exciting, even if at times it can be challenging. Recognising another's insensitivity may well be their personality trait and nothing actually to do with you, for example, can change your perspective. So if their thoughtless words or actions arise, as difficult as it can be at times, you are now more aware of their coping mechanism. You can then try not to take their behaviour so personally.

Being more authentic and aware of our coping mechanisms can help to enhance our relationships, and it may well get rid of a few! I had to let go of a couple of friends I had known for years after they were unpleasant and lacking in compassion whilst I was caring. They were often critical and opinionated – controlling but impassive. Steeped in the challenges of caring, I didn't have time for their self-centred and unpleasant behaviour. At times they cost me my peace, so I cut them loose, as my health and happiness were more important than pleasing them.

Carers often become so confined to their role and situation that they wonder if there is really any point in being authentic and opening up to others. What good is that going to do? If you feel like this, it is even more important to speak honestly with those around you. In doing so, you may even be pleasantly surprised, even liberated! This could then help lead you to living a more joyous life, even whilst caring.

Over to you...

- With whom can you be your most authentic? Who do you comfortably share your inner thoughts with, without fear of being judged? How important is this to you?

- Is anyone overstepping your boundaries? What do they say or do that puts upon you or undermines you? Could you speak to them and let them know how difficult you find their behaviour?

- Which 'shadow self', or selves, do you feel you mostly convey? Do you have any conflicts with others at present and, if so, can you recognise which archetypes they are?

- Could you make a commitment to yourself that, on a particular day or part of every day, you will be truly authentic with those around you? Could you share your inner thoughts openly whilst still being diplomatic? Notice how this makes you feel. If you do try this, does it then help your current situation?

5

Self-care is not selfish

Why would you need self-care? Surely, at present, a loved one needs your care right now. But it is essential not to forget your own health. This is not only important, it is in fact *vital*.

It can feel alien to many carers to focus on themselves because they are so used to giving care to another, but if you ignore your own health and fall ill, who is going to look after your loved one? Furthermore, who is going to look after *you?*

There is no glory in being a martyr and burning out

What is self-care?

When you have boarded a plane ready for take-off, you will probably have noticed the safety demonstrations shown by video or a flight attendant. They inform us that, if the oxygen levels drop during the flight, oxygen masks will fall from the cabin ceiling above us. We are then instructed to put on our *own* oxygen mask first, before helping anyone else, even if we have a baby or child with us. Why? If we don't place our mask on ourselves first, we are likely to lose consciousness and then we will be unable to help anybody else put on theirs.

The oxygen mask is a great metaphor for carers, as I have noticed they often leave their own oxygen masks dangling from the ceiling as they are too busy putting on everyone else's.

Self-care is very much like an oxygen mask. As a carer, you need to ensure you are safe, so that you are not only there for you, but also for your loved ones. If you are not safe, and something were to happen to you, not only could the cared-for be in jeopardy, but others would have to come to your rescue.

We need to be responsible for our own mental and physical health, especially whilst caring for another. This helps to reduce the negative psychological and physical effects of stress whilst caring. There is no glory in being a martyr and burning out. No one is going to appreciate it either, especially you. You may have many years ahead of you, so you need to make sure you remain fit and well to enjoy them.

Turning your love inwards

Be your own best-friend. If you have trouble with this, imagine if a good friend was going through what you are going through right now. What advice would you give them? We are often kinder to others than to ourselves. It's as if we don't believe we deserve to be happy. Our main priority is always someone else, but you are entitled to good health.

You can't pour from an empty cup.
Take care of yourself first

If your loved one has become accustomed to you consistently being there for them, over a period of time, your continued love and support can become expected or even taken for granted. If you then decide to take yourself off and do something for yourself, even for a short time, the cared-for may complain because anything different may make them feel uncomfortable or even vulnerable.

If you come up against resistance when looking to take time out, try reassuring your loved one that you are there for them, though you also need time for yourself. It's nothing personal, but you need space to recharge your batteries now and then. You can try explaining to them that in filling yourself up, you will then have more to give to them.

Enriching your life

Self-care is not just about brushing your teeth or taking a shower. It is also about enriching your own life – having and doing things that make you feel happy and fulfilled – enjoying pursuits that put a smile on your face and even may make you feel excited. These daily pleasures, however small, are really important. What do you enjoy doing? They say laughter is the best medicine and I love watching comedies. Laughter relieves physical stress in the body as well as cheering us up. If you have the internet, and you feel you need a laugh, you can click on www.YouTube.com and search for your favourite comedians or funny programmes. Within 10 minutes, you should notice a change in your mood. Just taking a few moments to do something you enjoy can help to break from an often monotonous routine – something many carers know about all too well.

Self-care for the body

As well as enriching your own life, self-care is also about taking care of your body – inside and out. Many carers cancel their own healthcare appointments because they do not have the time to break away from caring. It is vital to ensure you have your own health checks even if, sometimes, this can prove difficult. Maintaining your health is an imperative.

Also, caring for a loved one can be very physical. I put my

back out a number of times whilst moving and handling Neal. I almost passed out with the pain, which made it very difficult to continue caring. To manage this I would do some simple yoga stretches and back strengthening exercises. They are very simple but doing them little and often can help keep your back healthy. Search online or ask your local carers' centre if they offer classes to help support your back.

We can be adept at ignoring our physical symptoms – they can become part of the norm – but if we are not careful, these could worsen. Taking care of our bodies helps us to remain active, not only for our loved ones, but also for ourselves. Be aware of any aches and pains. They are your body signalling that you may need to do something about an underlying problem.

Caring for our appearance

If we are stuck at home caring all day, we may not feel inclined to pay attention to how we look, or we may just feel that there's not much point in spending time on ourselves.

As a woman, I know there is more to life than putting on make-up, but taking care of your appearance can make you feel better. I have a friend who works alone at home all day and some days I know she doesn't even bother to put a brush through her hair; she has told me she doesn't feel particularly great about it. This has then led her to not bothering to make herself something nice to eat that day. In failing to take care of herself at the beginning of the day, her lack of self-care has had a knock-on effect throughout the rest of it. Is this something you have ever noticed about yourself?

If it is, you may wonder to yourself, 'Why bother about how I look?' It only matters, if it matters to you. I just know that every morning, after showering and fixing my appearance, I feel happier and better prepared to face the day. Not only do I look my best for others, but for me, it shows I have a healthy respect for myself. It's not just a physical thing; it's a mental thing too.

Your emotional health is as important as your physical health. They go hand in hand. Make sure you have quality time to look after yourself. As good as it is to give love and care to others, it is equally good to give the same care and attention to yourself.

Over to you...

- Are you attending regular healthcare check-ups and appointments? It is important to go to these.

- Also, are you turning a blind eye to any worrying symptoms? If you notice any personal health issues, aches or pains, do not ignore them – let loved ones know and make an appointment to see your GP.

- What positive habits could you add to each day to give yourself care? A friend of mine would sit out in the garden for 10 minutes every day to read his newspaper. That was his time out, before embarking on the rest of the day. Not all carers may have time to do this, but are there moments in your day when you could add in activities to help you relax and enjoy the moment?

SECTION 2

Taking back control

6

Put the feelers out

Suddenly discovering you are a carer can be a daunting prospect. You may struggle to come to grips with the situation and the many challenges that can arise.

Many carers suffer loneliness and isolation, often because they are unable to leave their loved ones alone at home. Feelings of segregation can make us feel there is an invisible barrier between our own world and the world outside us. We might be thinking everyone else is enjoying their life whilst we have been forgotten. If we consistently have these negative thought patterns 'on a loop', this could lead to anxiety and depression. Not only this, many believe this is how life is now, and they just have to get on with it.

I believe life is what you make it, even during the most challenging times. Attempting to deal with caring solely on our own is not an option, but when it comes to looking for support, where do we turn? Sadly, there is not enough information or support for carers readily available. It took me years to discover the various channels open to support me as a carer, and support my disabled husband. The trouble is, how do you go looking for something you don't even know exists?

Most of us visit local doctors or hospitals when we fall ill, but, as I discovered, even though we visited these weekly, not once were we asked if we needed help at home or if we were getting enough support. There were times when it took all my effort to get Neal all the way to hospital for a regular appointment to see his oncologist, only for the consultant to treat our appointment as a 'ticking the box' exercise. Occasionally, as I reversed Neal in his wheelchair out of the consulting room, I have even laughed and asked, 'Is that it?'

Don't suffer in silence

To be honest, at that time, Neal was a palliative care patient and there was little more they could do for him, but even so, offering information on support at home would have been a great help.

During Neal's final year, his oncologist suggested we could Skype his appointment, saving us the stress of coming all the way to hospital, so that's what we did. If you don't have to have blood tests and are just having a follow-up appointment, you could suggest this to your doctor, provided they have the necessary facilities.

As our doctors didn't offer advice on where we could seek support, I had to put feelers out to discover what was available in our local area. Having done so, the help we finally received was wonderful and came from various sources, but I still had to go looking for it, on top of caring full-time.

The trouble is, how do you go looking for something you don't even know exists?

Many carers struggle behind closed doors. If this sounds like you, don't suffer in silence. You may have a carers' support centre nearby. I found mine invaluable. They informed me of other charities with help available to both Neal and me, also nearby. Where you live will determine what support is available to you.

There may be charities in your area that were originally founded for people with specific illnesses or conditions, but now also support those who care for them. There's no harm in calling them to find out if they can help. Even if they can't, they may know of other services in your area that could.

I have found that chatting with other carers at local charities helped me discover other services available. Other carers can provide a wealth of knowledge on what is available locally. Some years ago, a Macmillan Cancer Support specialist nurse visited Neal and me. She told us about a neurological charity down the road called Integrated Neurological Services (INS) that could support us both. Not only did INS give Neal one-to-one physiotherapy free of charge, but they supported me as his carer. I ended up as a trustee on their board, because I knew how important this charity was to families living with a disabled loved one with a neurological condition. You never know where an investigation may lead, what you could learn and even ultimately what you could give back. I remember one evening at an INS meeting, a retired man in his wheelchair with multiple sclerosis spoke honestly.

'After I was diagnosed, I sat at home and thought, well that's it, my life is over, but INS and their kindness and support have shown me that there is still much more living to do.'

He could have accepted his fate and remained at home, but discovered much more through the charity, which enriched his life. You just don't know what is available until you start looking. If you become involved with a charity, you may learn a whole lot more besides – things that could benefit both you and your loved one.

Charities and social services can give support as well as offering advice and pointing you in the direction of other available services. Check the posters and leaflets in your doctor's surgery or search online for 'local charity support' and don't feel bashful about receiving charity. Many charities are contracted or receive grants from the state to help in the community, so not all money comes from donations. There may also be local or national charities specific to your needs. In addition, look for day centres nearby that could give you a regular break for a number of hours whilst your loved one is looked after.

Carers can be a fountain of knowledge on what is available in your local area

You may have heard the phrase, 'If you don't ask, you don't get'. Opening up and speaking to your doctor, local services, friends, family and anyone else you can think of, could help you receive more support. If a district nurse or paid carers come to your home, they will be worth asking as well. You may be pleasantly surprised to find what is available for you.

Over to you...

Who can you reach out to?

- Do you have a local carers' centre and have you contacted it to see what is available for you and/or your loved one?

- Are there any other charities nearby that offer support to carers?

- Have you spoken to your doctor and healthcare specialists about what may be available to you from the state? Have you rung social services?

- If you search for charities in your local area online, are there any new charities or support groups that might be of benefit?

- Do you know of other carers you can reach out to, to discover what help and benefits they are receiving? Someone going through a similar situation to yours may have important information you would not have otherwise discovered.

7

Accepting change

If you have been caring for a while, you may have noticed considerable changes in your life. Firstly, your loved one's physical abilities and personality may have changed, as well as their appearance. Then, what you do on a day-to-day basis may also be different. Previously, you may have been working full-time but since your caring responsibilities have increased, you may either be working part-time or have given up your job and career altogether. This will then affect your income. Not only that, but you have probably had to change in order to cope with what is going on in your life.

When a loved one falls ill, they can become dependent on those around them. They may also feel vulnerable as their world becomes smaller. I think back to how strong and confident Neal was before his diagnosis, but years later he had become totally dependent on me. His personality changed from being an extrovert to becoming introverted and wanting to stay at home. He also lost confidence after his balance and walking deteriorated. His speech worsened and he could barely say a few words. This change was hard on both of us, as we missed our chats and laughter together. He was also unable to express how he was feeling, let alone tell me if he was in pain. As a result of all of this, our relationship inevitably changed. I ended up becoming more like his mother and nurse, rather than his wife.

I know of one carer whose husband was in a lot of pain. He was often very angry and spoke harshly towards her. I imagine this was at least partly due to the frustration of his condition and the discomfort. In turn, she continued to give him love and understanding every day. She clearly needed – and had – a lot of patience. We don't all make good patients.

If your loved one becomes angry and takes it out on you, try not to take it personally. Easier said than done, I know. Usually, this is because they don't know where to direct their distress and often it is the nearest and dearest who will take the full brunt of it. They may take it out on you, because they can. If this happens and becomes too much for you, let them know how it affects you. After all, you are not there to be an emotional punch bag.

When we are looking after a loved one, we may ask the question 'Why?' and spend a lot of time dwelling on it, but this will not help to resolve issues. We may feel sorry for ourselves and, if you do, I don't blame you, but for most of us, caring is a choice. I didn't have to care for Neal full-time. I could have put him in a home, but I'm glad I was there for him all those years. If you ask yourself, 'Why?' dig deeper and ask yourself, not why things are the way they are, but why you are caring for your loved one. You may have much deeper motivations, like wanting to alleviate your loved one's suffering. In caring for Neal, I'd like to think he would have been there for me, as I was for him. We can often give to others what we would want for ourselves.

Change is an inevitable part of life

One of the hardest things many carers have to deal with is the fact that their loved one could be gone at any moment. This can be very hard to accept and play on one's mind every day. If you are able to confide your feelings to close friends and family members, then do so, or, better still, if you are able to access counselling, then this is a good way to discuss your inner thoughts and accept what is happening at present. You could find you are grieving for the loss of your loved one before they have actually gone. When I knew Neal was living on borrowed time, I found this difficult to accept. I confided in close friends and would have a good cry. It's good to release those emotions. Try not to allow upsetting thoughts to continue to swirl around in your head, causing you continued pain.

Resisting what we cannot change will only increase our frustration. The psychologist, Carl Jung, once wrote, 'What you resist not only persists, but will grow in size.'

It is easy to focus on what we are not happy with, and to keep complaining about it – we all do – but this won't make the situation any easier or make us feel better. On the contrary, we are likely to feel worse.

Accept what you can't change and look for what you can. This will help to make your life easier. What do you have control over? For example, after regaining my health, I ensured I had control over it and, as mentioned previously, I would often go for a run as a way to alleviate stress and make myself feel better. I also had control over the household and the paid carers coming in to help me. On the other hand, I didn't have control over Neal's worsening condition and I had to accept this. We cannot control everything.

Allow yourself to notice your feelings. At times, the majority of carers can feel upset, resentful and even angry at the lack of support or understanding from friends, family and healthcare professionals. These negative emotions are natural and they just mean you are human. Not everyone will understand what you are going through. I am a very positive person but I certainly experienced many dark and negative feelings whilst caring.

There will always be change in life, whether good or bad.

Nothing stays the same forever, even if you feel your life is on hold at present.

Acknowledge where you are now, and what is going on around you. Accept what you can't change and look for what you can. This can help make life more bearable and easier to manage. Determining what you can do to regain some control will help to put you on a better path to alleviate needless suffering.

Not all change is bad

One big change I noticed about myself during my caring years, was that I became a lot more patient. Getting worked up, angry and frustrated took up a whole lot of time and energy, which I didn't have to lose. I finally realised there was no point in getting het up and making myself feel worse. I came to terms with, and accepted, the situation, which made life easier to bear – not only for myself, but, also for Neal who then didn't have to put up with such an exasperated wife.

What we resist, persists

I think the biggest change for both of us came when Neal's physical abilities drastically changed. He became unable to speak, but he was still able to give a thumbs-up with his right hand – a great positive signal. If I asked him if he would like a chocolate brownie, his favourite treat, his thumb would go up in 0.2 seconds. Although he could hardly communicate, this gesture was clearly one of enthusiasm and an endearing memory for me. As challenging as life can become, try surrendering to what is and allowing it to wash over you. This can then help you to focus on the positives to enjoy each day.

If your loved one has slowed or their mobility has waned, rushing them will just stress you both out. Trying to get them ready quickly for an appointment, when you're already late, can cause you both grief. Your loved one may not be able to speed up, but you can certainly slow down. If you are noticing this, factor in more time to allow the cared-for to go at *their* pace, which will make for an easier day for you both.

Meet them in a place where they are

Whoever you care for, accept where *they* are right now. This will make a situation easier, as well as making them feel better.

There will be some things which are uncomfortable to accept. If the cared-for refuses to go to the doctor about a certain problem, or refuses to talk about something, we may just have to accept it. It is *their* body and *their* life, difficult though this can be for us. We can only offer our love and advice. If they refuse to take it, then that is their choice. A few years ago, my uncle, who'd had pain in his chest for months, refused to see his doctor. His wife, a nurse, tried to talk him round to seeing a specialist, but this never happened. Sadly, one morning after he arrived at work, he had a heart attack and died. It was a shock to his family, as he was so young. He'd had so much more life to live. As much as my aunt had wanted him to see a doctor, she couldn't force him. It was his choice and one we had to accept, difficult as it was.

The messy side of caring

Should your loved one become incontinent, it can be a messy and unpleasant business. Neal became incontinent over night and it was a shock for both of us. The bed or sofa would suddenly be soaked in urine and I would spend a lot of time cleaning him, and the furniture, up. I found this time stressful and would vocalise it rather loudly. Not very nice for Neal, as it was not his fault. During the early years of Neal's incontinence, I would describe myself as 'a bit of a shouty wife'. I showed little empathy for him, who could only sit and listen to my tirade.

I then realised how I must have sounded to him and I sat down and apologised. He couldn't help it and it must have been awful for him. I told him how much I loved him, that it wasn't his fault and that I was frustrated due to the situation – not him. From then on, I told him, I would do my best to keep calm whenever it happened again. Eventually, I accepted his incontinence and there were no further outbursts. Not long after this I managed to knock a full bottle of urine onto the living room carpet. You would be amazed by my self-restraint. I certainly was! Surrendering to the inevitable made life easier for us both.

There can be many hardships whilst caring, and I found the smaller things in life that used to bother me became less important. You come to realise what really matters, and what does not. So, try not to sweat the small stuff; you are doing something remarkable – caring for another.

Another change carers often experience, if they care full-time from home, is finding that their world has become smaller. So, whenever opportunities arise to allow you to leave the house, make the most of them. Try not to feel guilty leaving your loved one and make space for some 'me time'. In the early days I would remain at home with Neal throughout the week because I knew that was what he preferred. In the end, it didn't do either of us any good because I would become tired and frustrated. I needed a break. I then felt better to continue caring.

Over to you...

- Try making a list of what you can't change and then a list of what you can. What changes can you make for the better?

- Have you noticed yourself reacting to a particular experience negatively, by being upset with the cared-for or with family? Or have you been angry with a poor service you may have been receiving? Could you have dealt with this differently, so as to have achieved a better result? What could you do next time?

- Have you noticed any negative changes in yourself whilst caring – for example, regularly feeling low or irritable, or suffering from a bad back? What could you do to help improve this? Who could you turn to?

- Some carers distract themselves from their situation by being overly busy. For example, you may vacuum the house every day, even though the floors are already spotless. Is there anything that takes up your valuable time that acts as a distractor? As I mentioned in my story earlier in the book, my distractor was drinking alcohol. If you notice you have a particular distractor that does not serve you, could you do something else in its place that would be better for you?

- Have you changed in a positive way whilst caring? Have you learnt anything new or do you do anything differently that makes life easier?

8

Rise to the challenge

Life's challenges are good for us. They can drive us forward and expand our knowledge. Caring for someone is a huge life challenge from which we can learn a lot, although the challenge of caring should never be underestimated. Not everyone can be a carer – well, not a good one. It takes perseverance, patience, inner strength and, above all, love.

Years ago, if someone had told you you'd one day become a carer, what would you have thought? Previously, you might have assumed it didn't sound like much. Maybe you would have thought a carer was a kind of 'dogsbody' for someone needing help? However, if you were now to list everything you actually do in your caring role, and what it entails, your earlier self would probably have fallen sideways to hear it. Not only are you filling the important role as an emotional and physical rock to another, but there will be other commitments too, and sometimes your chores can feel endless.

Often, the carer has to take over tasks the cared-for used to do and cannot do any longer due to their deterioration. For example, one morning I found myself attempting to mow the lawn with Neal's petrol lawnmower because he was too unwell to do this anymore. The grass was now half a metre high. As I attempted to start his petrol mower by pulling the very long pull-cord fast into the air, in one quick movement, I strained all the muscles down one side of my body. Neal would have undoubtedly found it easy to start the engine, being twice my size, but I found it very difficult and it took quite a few attempts to get the old metal contraption working. I had enough to deal with, and now I had grass-cutting to add to my ever-growing list of things to do. That old mower ended up down at the dump, as I didn't want to hurt myself further, and I treated myself to a new electric one.

As we continue to care, our challenges can change over time. When Neal was first diagnosed, my priority was to support him emotionally and keep him going, whilst driving him to hospital for treatment each week. During this time, I would also look for second opinions and alternative therapies to help improve his health. Years later, the challenges changed considerably and became more physical. After he became disabled, I needed to learn how to hoist him out of bed and into a wheelchair. A few years after this, my challenge was to learn how to administer medicines and food via a feeding tube and keep it clean in case of infection. There was always something new to learn.

Although my challenges seemed to build in a series of increments, for some carers change can be drastic, such as a loved one becoming disabled over night following a stroke. Although this will be exceptionally challenging, taking one day at a time will help you not only to master the situation, but also to weather the storm. Also, remember to be kind to yourself. You can only do your best. As we learn, we grow and life eventually becomes easier.

Take one day at a time,
to help you weather the storm

Have you had to adapt or learn new skills whilst caring? When you think back, how much have you learnt since then?

Carers have to learn a plethora of information, procedures and terminology in order to ensure their loved one receives the right care and support.

Most carers also have to learn the hard way, on their own. When we received Neal's first wheelchair, there was no lap restraint on it, and unbeknown to me, this was dangerous. Neal was a big, heavy man. One day, as one of his friends took over pushing him along the side of a rugby pitch, an underlying bump bounced Neal straight out of his wheelchair. Luckily, he wasn't hurt but he was clearly annoyed. Until then, I hadn't realised how important a lap restraint was. You would think the wheelchair services would have known this. I then ensured one was added as soon as possible.

A change of attitude makes a big difference

When I found caring challenging, I would often use a bit of humour to see me through the day. It would tickle me and help me to keep me going. Because Neal was nearly double my weight, I would often describe moving and handling him, whilst pushing him in his wheelchair, as 'the Challice Workout'.

Neal used to use a particular phrase, 'No good deed goes unpunished!' when I became exasperated whilst caring for him. This would always make us both chuckle.

Telomeres tell a lot

We all have a choice as to how to deal with life's challenges. New research has come to light on how the way we perceive the challenge of caring can affect our health.

There are particular markers in our bodies called telomeres. Telomeres are caps of DNA at the ends of chromosomes that protect our cells from ageing. They can be described as being like the glue at the end of a shoelace. Our telomeres are a certain length when we are born and, as we age, they gradually shorten. Research has shown that the length of our telomeres signifies how much life we have left to live. They are a mark of our ageing.

The Nobel Prize-winning biologist, Elizabeth Blackburn, researched the course of telomeres, with a particular study. She measured the length of telomeres in mothers caring for chronically ill children. She then discovered that the more these mothers perceived their situation as being stressful, the shorter their telomeres became. The continued chronic stress of caring had aged many of them.

It must be very difficult to care for a chronically ill child, and more so in the knowledge that the stress of caring may have impacted your own health, but in this study, there was hope. Some of the mothers' telomeres had retained the normal length for their age. How had this happened?

After interviewing the mothers with healthy telomere lengths, it was discovered that they had not regarded their circumstances as a threat day in and day out. Instead, they had viewed their circumstances as a challenge. Their resilient and upbeat attitude to their situation had safeguarded the length of their telomeres and, in turn, their own health and longevity.

Another study from the University of California, Los Angeles, looked at the length of telomeres in carers who looked after loved ones with dementia. The carers were asked to meditate for as little as 12 minutes a day for two months. The study found that meditation actually improved the length of the telomeres. This research revealed that even though stress whilst caring could shorten telomeres, and hence longevity, taking time to meditate could actually reverse this shortening.

I am aware not everyone is keen on meditating, and it can be difficult to quieten your mind and switch off your brain, but there are many great guided meditations out there. I personally enjoy Dr Joe Dispenza's guided meditations, but there are many which are free of charge on various websites, including YouTube, plus there are Apps, some of which are free, which you can download onto your smart phone, such as *Calm*.

If you rise to the challenge of caring for a loved one, rather than regarding it as a hardship, you are more likely to find it manageable, as well as learning and experiencing more about life. When we are challenged, we learn, we grow and we evolve. You may well have heard the phrase, 'What doesn't kill you, makes you stronger'. We certainly don't want caring to finish us off, but we certainly do learn whilst we care. Also, caring for another can give our lives a greater sense of purpose. It can be a course in real-life experience, so long as we don't allow it to overwhelm us.

To make life easier, we may need to adapt to the many changes which can occur whilst caring

The fight-or-flight response

Continuous chronic stress can wreak havoc with our health. Carers are often, unknowingly, in fight-or-flight response mode, also known as the 'acute stress response'. Many generations ago, when our ancestors faced imminent danger, such as from predatory wild animals, their bodies would go into a state of high alert and, to ensure their safety, they would have to decide in a split second whether to fight, freeze or flee. Their body's sympathetic nervous system would prompt the release of adrenaline. This increases heart rate, blood pressure and breathing rate, giving the body the best chance of surviving. This is useful if a predator is on your tail, but not if your body is continuously stuck in the fight-or-flight mode on a daily basis, when there is nothing to flee from. Carers can become stuck in the fight-or-flight response due to the daily stresses of caring. This aroused state and daily adrenaline rush can then feel normal.

Being stuck in the fight-or-flight response is like putting your foot on the accelerator and brake pedals at the same time. Adrenaline continuously pumps through your body, even though there's no immediate physical danger. This constant level of stress can lead to symptoms such as rapid heartbeat, pale or flushed skin and trembling; and even panic attacks. You may remember the story in Section One (page 5) of Pam who endured a panic attack. Continuous stress can also suppress your immune system, leaving you susceptible to illness. Have you noticed yourself regularly catching a cold or feeling generally run-down? If so, your immune system may be low, so look for ways to relax and calm yourself. To take your mind off your current situation you could read a good book, or go outside for some fresh air. You could even find a new goal to keep your mind occupied. I know a lovely carer in her 70s who did just that. For many years, Paula cared for her husband with Parkinson's disease. Although she was retired and caring full-time, she trained at her local adult education college as a reflexologist. Not only did Paula learn a new skill, taking her mind off the caring, but she would use this therapy to help her husband and alleviate his symptoms. She finally offered reflexology to other carers at her local carers' centre, helping them to relax. I was one of those lucky enough to receive her therapy. She was a real inspiration.

See each challenge as a chance to grow

As long as you don't overwhelm yourself, setting goals can give you something to strive for and take your mind off the monotony of caring. It can keep your mind stimulated and engaged.

Over to you...

- Now you know you have the power to shorten or lengthen your telomeres – key markers of ageing – how would you feel if you knew your telomeres were shorter than they should be? What plans would you put in place so as to reduce your stress levels, helping to safeguard your telomeres and your health?

- What activities do you enjoy that could help to take your mind off your present situation?

- Are there any goals you could set yourself to keep your mind or body active? Is there anything new you would like to learn?

9

For love or obligation?

Why do you care?

Why do you care for your loved one? Do you do it because you have to, or because you want to? If you are caring for your spouse, you may feel it is compulsory after taking your wedding vow, 'in sickness and in health'. If so, do you regard caring as love or as an obligation? Possibly both? If you feel you are caring solely out of obligation, do you think this is a good enough reason to give it your time, your energy, even your life?

You may feel that caring is something you do instinctively and you haven't even asked yourself this question. After all, your loved one needs help and if you didn't care, who would?

We would certainly like to think we live in a caring society and that if we ourselves were to fall ill, somebody would love us enough to ensure we were looked after. Not only this; it is also healthy for our society to care for our vulnerable.

A few years back, I was at a music gig with three friends. I almost didn't attend, because I had hurt my back whilst caring and we were booked to be in the standing area. My brother was working at the stadium at the time, and he arranged for us to have seats near the back. As we settled to watch the performance, I happened to chat to a woman in her 30s who was part of the security staff. She knew my brother and he had told her of my circumstances. As I briefly told her the story of why I was injured, she told me her husband was also long-term sick due to a brain tumour. They had two children and she admitted she had struggled with the caring and finally walked away from her marriage, taking their children with her. She told me she couldn't cope with his illness on top of everything else and wanted to live a 'normal' life.

At the time, I was surprised by her honesty in sharing her story. I also found it a shame that she had made this decision, but I then quickly realised it was not for me to judge. I didn't know the full circumstances. Before his illness, had they had a good relationship? Did she love him? Also, I had heard of some brain tumours causing alterations to personality, dependent upon where the tumour sat in the brain. Furthermore, when some of us fall ill, we can make for a very difficult patient. So, there could have been a whole host of other issues before or arising from her loved one's illness that had made her walk away. Finally, as I've mentioned previously, some of us just don't make good carers.

What if you were to stop right now and walk away from your caring responsibilities? You can, you know. I know it sounds heartless, but caring is a choice. When I was at the end of my tether and social services had done me more harm than good, I threatened to wheel Neal up to their offices and let them have a go at looking after him. They had persistently let me down and I felt, ironically, that they didn't care. I may have only threatened, but I needed to make the point. They were meant to be there for the vulnerable in the community. If they didn't care, why should I?

Caring _is_ a choice

Although I argue that caring is a choice, and that we don't have to care, there will always be repercussions if we turn our back. Whilst I was caring, I made a friend at our local gym. He shared his story of how his sister had fallen long-term sick many years before, back in his home country. With tears in his eyes, he told me how he could have been there for her. He could have helped once in a while and offered his love and support, but he chose not to and turned a blind eye. He left other family members to look after her until she passed away. He regretted not visiting regularly to spend quality time with her and now she was gone. He felt he had abandoned her and realised that we only have so much time with our loved ones, especially if they become unwell. He was aware he could have done more but, instead, he had kept away and left other family members to look after her. He felt he had not only let his sister and family down, but he had let himself down as well.

Caring out of love is very different, in fact poles apart, from caring out of obligation. If you are caring because you feel you have to, your loved one may very well pick up on this. Apparently, at least 80% of human communication is non-verbal. That means it's not just what we say, but how we say it. Also, gestures and expressions are part of communication, and most of us cannot hide our feelings. So, if you feed, wash or dress another begrudgingly, they will sense it. How would you feel if you were poorly and a family member resentfully came to help get you dressed and washed in the morning? You would be aware that they did not want to be there – were only helping you because they felt they had to. How would this make you feel? Probably, even lower. You would already be ill, but on top of this you would feel like a burden as well. If you are experiencing such negative emotions, is it going to help with your recovery?

Even if we are caring out of love, we can slowly be ground down by the responsibilities. At times it ground me down. Most of the time I cared with love, but there were moments of pure frustration, and I would notice this click into obligation mode. Particularly when my back hurt and I felt exhausted, I noticed my tone of voice change and, with it, Neal's experience of receiving my care. Over time, I came to recognise when my attitude had changed for the worse. I would take a break and then continue caring, or else I would make a concerted effort to change it for the better.

If you find you are caring out of frustration and you can feel it not doing either you or your loved one any good, try taking a break from the situation if you possibly can.

In the end, I gave Neal the care I would want for myself. I knew the illness had worn him down. It wore us both down! So, I wanted to make him as comfortable as possible. I cared out of love, and in doing so it made me feel much better. This put me in a better frame of mind. I then became more relaxed and more in control of the situation.

Once in a while, Neal went into a hospice for a week to give me a break. When he returned home, he was usually not as good as when he had left, but within a day or so he would clearly be better. Why was this? He was never keen to go into the hospice, but I believe his health improved on his return because he was in the comfort of his own home, cared for, loved and wanted.

Caring out of love can be beneficial for both of you

Even when you do your best and care with great love, it may not always be reciprocated. If your loved one is in chronic pain or loathes being unwell, they may take out their frustration on their nearest and dearest – you! Also, if they have a neurological condition, like Alzheimer's, they may not realise what they are doing.

In Neal's last four years, he could rarely speak, but once in a while he would manage to say a couple of words. After months of silence, he suddenly spoke up one day. At the time I was perched on the edge of his bed, feeding him chocolate mousse. Were his words full of love and of gratitude for all that I had done for him? No, he said, 'I hate you.'

I was completely taken aback and felt really hurt. I stopped feeding him and looked at him in disbelief. In a slightly cross tone I said,

'Have you got any idea what I do for you, Neal? Every day? Do you know what I have given up to look after you?'

Because he couldn't really move, his only expression came from his eyes, which went really wide. He didn't say anything more. He couldn't. In those moments, not only was he disabled from a brain tumour, but he now had a disgruntled wife to contend with. I didn't say much more and carried on feeding him.

That evening I went up to bed in tears. I had given him my all and I felt it had been thrown back in my face. As I sat quietly on the side of my bed, contemplating the situation, I began to reflect on how *he* was feeling. There was only one person in the world he could take his anger and frustration out on – me. He might also have been voicing pent up resentment, because I was able-bodied and able to leave the house and see friends, something Neal would never be able to do again. Or else, maybe he wanted to push me away to go and live my life. He knew I was very low sometimes when caring for him, though I could only speculate. He never said those words again.

Do I think Neal really hated me at that time? Looking back, I don't think he did. It was the only way he could express how he was feeling. The next day, I made it clear to him that I loved him. At that time, I recognised my unconditional love for him. I would be there for him, whatever it took.

So, if your loved one says or does something that upsets you, try to understand the place they are coming from, even if sometimes you feel like an emotional punch bag. Their behaviour may not be entirely in character, especially if they are suffering. They may just be letting off steam. Difficult as it may be, try not to take it personally.

Caring can put pressure on other relationships in your life. Friends and family know that you care, but they may still cause you grief without realising they are adding to your stress levels. I have certainly found myself appeasing family and friends whilst being overwhelmed with caring. I would say 'Yes' to something that family had asked of me when, in hindsight, I didn't have the capacity or even want to do it. I then did it out of obligation.

Imagine you want to go out for the day and have asked a friend to join you. Now imagine your friend does not really want to come but has said 'Yes' to appease you. So, you both head off for your day out, but all the time your friend really doesn't want to be there. If you were to discover that they had come with you purely out of obligation, how would you feel? Would you still have wanted them to come with you? Your friend will have lived that day as a lie – they weren't being true to themselves or truthful with you. It is not comfortable when you discover someone isn't honest with you. It also makes them appear weak because they are afraid of speaking their mind. They would rather keep quiet and make you happy than be honest.

If we try to be whatever everyone else wants us to be, we are living a life that is not our own. We are trying to meet others' expectations to live as they think we should. We betray ourselves. As a result, we can become stressed or even depressed when we wake up one day and discover our life is not our own.

Do you put yourself last in the pecking order? If so, find time to please yourself. When I have left myself last, I have become low as a result. The amusing thing is that all those around me didn't seem to be the slightest bit grateful for my continual effort. By trying to please everyone, I would end up pleasing no one, especially not myself. If this is happening to you, try taking back control, empowering yourself and being honest with those around you. Don't allow yourself to be taken for granted.

Striking a balance of being there for our loved ones, whilst ensuring we spend time on ourselves, will help us to feel more in control of our lives and to recharge our batteries. We shall then have more to give to others, as we shall be living our lives on our own terms.

It can take courage to be honest with those around us, especially if we don't know how they will react. When speaking the truth, try being diplomatic, as we don't need to upset anyone, but we do want them to understand. They may not be entirely happy, but we only have so much energy to give and caring for another can take up quite enough of it.

Loving and respecting yourself will help you make the right decisions

Asking yourself the simple question, 'Am I doing this out of love or obligation?' will help you to navigate your choices and understand whether you are doing something for the right reasons.

Over to you...

- Have you noticed whether you are caring out of love or obligation? When you care out of love, do you notice how it feels, compared with caring because you have to?

- If you feel you are mostly caring more out of obligation, do you need to be there? Can someone else take over or help? Imagine if the roles were reversed and the cared-for were begrudgingly looking after you, would you want them to continue caring for you?

- What positive reasons do you have for caring for your loved one? Meaningful motivation can help us through tough times.

- Try looking at the situation in a different way. Endeavour to do each task with love and see how it feels.

- In between chores, relax and do something for yourself, even for a short while. We all need regular breaks from caring. If we become exhausted, frustration and resentment can easily take over.

- Are there times when you agree to do something for friends, family or work colleagues, when really you wanted or needed to say 'No'? In retrospect, if the situation arose again, what would you say or do differently?

10

Straight talking

Straight talking – easily enough said, right? So why can it be so difficult? Communication is key, especially if we are not happy with the way some things are and we need more support. A lot of carers keep their true feelings close to their chest, not letting others know how they really feel. This can happen for a few reasons. We may do this to avoid letting others worry, or upsetting someone, or it may be that we do not want to appear as though we are not coping. We may also be fearful of what others might say and how they might judge us. I know at times I needed more support, but did I say anything?

As I slowly became ill from the stress of caring, whenever a family member rang and asked how I was, I always replied with the same words, 'I'm fine, thanks,' even though I knew I was not.

As mentioned in the chapter, 'Drop the mask,' I was putting on a brave face. I also thought the enquirer had little empathy, so why bother telling them how I really was? On the other hand, if they didn't know I wasn't coping, how would they know whether to offer their help? Sometimes, we have to either manage or guide others to helping us, so we don't end up in a crisis situation.

Whilst caring, I had a number of issues with a family member who could have helped me with caring for Neal. I mentioned this to a friend. She told me to open up and be honest with this person, then maybe they would offer more help. It's marvellous isn't it? You have enough to contend with as a carer, but then you have to deal with other family relationships in an attempt to bring them onto your side.

Finally, I plucked up the courage to speak to them over the phone and I told them how they made me feel. I needed them to know because, if I continued falling ill from lack of support, Neal would probably end up dying in a nursing home.

I loathe confrontations, so, to get my point across in a diplomatic way, and to ensure they got the message, I decided to *write down* exactly how I wanted the conversation to go and what points I wanted to make. There had been problems with this person over the years, and if I wanted to come clean and have an honest conversation, it would be best to have it all out in the open at one time. If I became flustered during the conversation, I could always revert to the points I had written down.

A few days later, ensuring I had the piece of paper with all I needed to say in front of me, I spoke to them over the phone and made my feelings known. During the call, I remained calm, taking emotion out my voice, even though I found this hard. Years of unhappiness came down to this one phone call. I didn't want upset and anger to get in the way of the real issues which needed addressing in asking for more support. I also didn't want to fall out with family. It wasn't an easy conversation, but having all I wanted to say written down in front of me helped guide me through, ensuring they received the message.

Take the pressure off yourself – let them know

How did the problem person respond? Well, they were surprised and a bit upset. They asked me if I wanted them to come each week. I didn't need them to come that often, but I did want help now and then, instead of it all being left to me. I just needed them to know how things really were and to appreciate all that I did.

After our conversation, I felt better. Now they knew how I really felt. Although nerve-racking, letting others know how you really feel can help take the pressure off yourself. It is unhealthy to bottle up negative thoughts and feelings, brought on by difficult relationships. They just add another layer of stress. Also, by speaking to the person concerned, you are putting the ball in their court and you just never know – maybe they will do something about it. Even if they don't, at least they will be aware of how you are feeling.

Now, after I had plucked up the courage to open up, did this family member come and help me? Not really, although I did notice their attitude slightly change for the better. People are not suddenly going to change just because you want them to. However, I found the technique of writing my points down before having a tricky conversation really useful, and I have used it a few times since, when I have needed to get my point across during a difficult conversation.

So many carers accept their fate and struggle on, instead of banging a drum and asking for more help. A male carer once told me that if he had done just one thing differently over those many years of caring for his wife, it would have been to ask for more help. I asked him why he had not. He admitted he hadn't wanted to look as though he had failed. We all need help from time to time. When we are struggling and not coping well, we need to seek help from friends and family, or from local services, before things worsen. Not everyone will be supportive, but I believe many carers would fare better to be more honest and direct when asking for help. Still too many of us are not.

Just as it is important to communicate effectively with family when in need of more support, it is also imperative that we make our feelings known to the services we receive in our community if they have let us down.

Neal spent two months in hospital after a stroke. His time there was supposedly stroke-rehabilitation. Sadly, we felt that this was not the case. There were many failings and he was badly injured due to their lack of care. He deteriorated quickly during the six weeks on the ward. The few doctors, who rarely spoke to me during that time, even though I was there every day, only kept repeating that Neal was a DNR (Do Not Resuscitate). They had clearly given up on him and expected the worst.

As Neal was so poorly, and the outlook was bleak, I did not want him dying in hospital, so I organised for him to be brought home as soon as possible. I wanted him in the comfort of his home with loved ones, especially if these were to be his last weeks.

A few days after he was brought home, along with a hoist and hospital bed, he clearly improved. It was such a relief, although he was still severely disabled and needed 24/7 nursing care. The dreadful failings of the hospital, leading to Neal's suffering, were etched onto my mind. I was angry and I felt they needed to know, but my nursing chores took over and it was left by the wayside.

A year later, I was at a local carers' event and sat next to a lady whose husband had also been in the same hospital. She told me of their similar dreadful experiences which had only recently happened. I couldn't believe this was still going on. The following day, as Neal's district nurse paid a visit, I mentioned this to her. She told me that it was never too late to complain, and that I should let them know. I realised that, because Neal was unable to speak after his stroke, I was his voice. If he was harmed in any way, it was down to me to make sure this was known.

The hospital had a PALS (Patient Advice and Liaison Service), and I emailed them a long list of all the failings over those dreadful few months.

If you have experienced difficulties whilst at a hospital, you may have a PALS or something similar to contact. PALS offer confidential advice, support and information on health-related matters and are a point of contact for patients, their families and carers. They also deal with any complaints you may have within the hospital; they were my 'go to' for Neal's experience on the stroke ward.

Vocalise your feelings and be direct in asking for help

A few weeks later, PALS came back to me and asked if I would consider coming in for a meeting with the management and staff of the stroke ward about the issues I had raised. I wasn't overly keen on meeting the staff face-to-face and telling them of their failures, but I knew it needed to be done, so I agreed and the date was set.

Confronting the staff during a two hour meeting wasn't comfortable. They were open to my comments and spoke of the issues from their side. The particular issue that had meant Neal had been physically harmed had since been addressed; consequently, other patients wouldn't endure the same kind of injury. Although the meeting was awkward, I'm glad I went through with it. I had spoken not only for Neal, but also for anyone else who had suffered in that ward. Also, if Neal suffered, I suffered. If he was in pain, it emotionally affected and drained me. I even remember feeling faint one afternoon, as he lay groaning in pain for hours. He had been through enough, and so had I.

If you are empathic, able to perceive another's emotions, and your loved one was in pain due to negligence, I am sure you would also find the experience draining. So, when I complained about the lack of care, I was also complaining about the emotional pain I had endured in the process.

Carers and their loved ones use many services, including local hospitals, care agencies, GPs, district nurses and transport, to name but a few. Some provide a fantastic service and are much appreciated, but this is not always the case. If a service is poor, communication is key. How are they going to improve if they are not aware of the problems? Any services you receive should not be there to burden you. They are there to make your life easier.

I like to think that if a service lets us down, we let them know, not just for ourselves, but for everyone else in our community who may also be experiencing similar difficulties. To put it another way, I am pretty sure they are not saving that poor service just for you.

If you notice a service you are receiving is going downhill, you may find it useful to jot down the details. Then, if the problem continues over the coming weeks and months, you have everything to hand, making it easier for you to give feedback. I found this useful after a care agency had let us down again and again. There was no way I would remember every single detail over those months. Logging each problem – who, when, where and the issue – not only made feedback easier when the time arose, but allowed for a more detailed and constructive complaint when emailing the information. Also, one thing that is good to note when logging a problem is the knock-on effects. If you have been let down, what did this mean for you and the cared-for? Did it add more stress? Did it cause more problems? These details can help to strengthen a complaint.

Communicating a problem is the first step to putting it right

Another time, Neal was physically harmed after another

hospital stay. He came home with marks all over his body due to the lack of care from healthcare professionals. I took photos of the wounds, to make this documented evidence as you never know when you might need to produce it. Jotting down details, taking photos or collecting any relevant evidence, when there appears to be an ongoing problem with a poor service, can only make it easier for ourselves when we need to give feedback.

Communicating effectively will help others become aware of any problems that may have arisen. This is the first step in putting it right. If you are doing your best, surely they should be doing theirs? Hopefully, then, life becomes more manageable.

Over to you...

- Are there any particular friend or family issues you have at present?
    - o Are the problem people aware of how you feel? If they are not, why not write down what you would like to say to them? Is it possible to have a chat with them over the phone and make your points in a relaxed and diplomatic way?
    - o If you were to chat with them, what would you like the end result to be? Complaining to them might just get their back up, which would not help you. If they asked you how they could help, what would you like them to do?
    - o If you are asking them to do something in particular – such as to sit with your loved one whilst you take a break – could you ask this in a positive way? For example, 'I would really appreciate it if you could come and look after

[name] for a few hours whilst I take a break, because at present I am exhausted and struggling to cope.' It's worth asking. You just never know.

- If you or your loved one receive any services which you feel may be below par, start making a record of what you are unhappy with and ask who you need to contact to resolve the matter.

- Are there any other carers you know who are also experiencing similar difficulties with a particular service? It's good to come together to have our voices heard. There is strength in numbers.

11

Are you too caring?

It is important to have kindness and compassion whilst caring because this helps you gain a better understanding of what your loved one's needs are and how you can meet them. Many carers have love and understanding and furthermore are empaths. This means they are highly sensitive and feel the emotional states of others. Having empathy can be an asset whilst caring, because this allows you to sense how a loved one is feeling. As useful as this is, absorbing another's emotional and physical pain can, at times, be draining.

Empaths don't have the same filters as other people. Crowds can leave empaths exhausted and particular people may drain them. They often need time to relax after a busy day and they are often highly sensitive and easily upset. Does any of this sound like you?

My friend, Pauline, has cared for her husband for nearly 30 years – a long time. He is now very disabled from a neurological condition. Once in a while, Pauline and I meet up for a coffee to catch up. One morning, whilst sitting with our cuppa, I asked her how she was. Pauline is in her 60s and her health, including her walking, has deteriorated. Even so, her focus is rarely on herself, but on others. Firstly, she told me about her husband's health issues. Next, she moved on to a friend who had cancer. Awful news! I continued to listen. She then informed me of an older man who cared for his wife and had refused to have surgery because he dared not leave her. Finally, she shared the story of another lady whose son had committed suicide. These were all distressing accounts of people who were suffering. As she continued with the list of sick or dying people, I reached out and touched her arm.

'I know there are lots of people going through a lot of awful stuff, Pauline, but what about you? How are *you* doing?'

Pauline briefly discussed her own health, but moments later she was talking of another person who was confronting health challenges. Again, I reached out and put my hand on her arm to try and bring her around to talking about herself. I wanted to know how her health was and if she had done anything enjoyable lately. Had she had any days or evenings out over the last few months? As her attention drifted back onto others, I kept trying to guide her back to her own life, but she couldn't stop thinking and worrying about others, even though she had her own health problems as well as caring for a poorly and disabled man.

Pauline is a great empath, but I feel she has too much empathy for others, which stops her from focusing on her own wants and needs, or from enjoying her time out in the coffee shop with her friend. I worry about Pauline's health (another empath!), because she now has pain whilst walking. Even though she has enough to deal with, she gives too much of herself to others, agonising over their pain and suffering.

During our conversation, I also noticed Pauline seemed to be on a loop, going around and around others in need. Have you noticed yourself doing this? If you have, understand that there is only so much you can do for anyone. We may allow ourselves to have that impulse to help someone in need, as long as we don't leave ourselves depleted.

There can be benefits to being an empath. For example,

even if the cared-for doesn't vocalise how they are feeling, you can sense their emotions. This was useful in our case, when my husband became unable to speak, as I usually knew what he needed; I was then able to make him as comfortable as possible.

Some empaths cannot differentiate between others' emotions and their own. Imagine caring for someone with chronic pain. Now imagine this pain as a heavy weight that you carry around all day, along with your own emotions. This heavy burden will eventually have you floored. If you notice yourself taking on another's mental or physical suffering, find time and space for yourself every day, away from others. It doesn't need to be for long, but just enough to help you re-centre and recharge your batteries.

In giving our love and kindness, we all like to think that our caring makes a positive impact on another, but what if you are caring for someone with a progressive disorder like multiple sclerosis or Parkinson's disease? It doesn't matter how much love you give them, they will sadly eventually decline. Putting all my love into Neal whilst he continued to deteriorate made me, at times, feel like despairing. I felt myself sinking with him. This is when I realised I needed to take time out and recognise there was only so much I could do. We can give our cared-for our love, but we have no control over the outcome. That is why caring can be so very difficult.

Co-dependency

Being over-empathetic to others could prevent you from living your own life. If we are not careful, this can also create a co-dependent relationship with the cared-for. Co-dependency means responding automatically to others' needs and bypassing your own. The knock-on effect may mean that the cared-for does not help him/herself as much as they could, because the carer is doing everything for them. In turn, the carer is so busy fulfilling the cared-for's needs, that they stop focusing on their own life and their own needs.

I recently interviewed a carer, Laura, who was young, intelligent and divorced, bringing up two sons on her own. She had cared for her mother who had suffered from severe depression for many years but, following a diagnosis of breast cancer, her mother had sadly died. Her father was now becoming elderly and had mobility issues. He lived alone, so Laura had moved him in with her family to keep an eye on him. When I asked Laura what she really wanted to do with her life, she enthusiastically told me she had always wanted to be a counsellor. To qualify, she would need to go on a course and pass exams. I asked her when she was to start her studies. She shook her head.

'I can't,' she replied. 'Dad might worsen and would need me.'

Laura's father was still able to care for himself, heading out for an afternoon or going to the shops. He didn't need supervision and was capable of looking after himself, even if he was becoming older. However, after he had moved into her family home, she felt he had become more reliant on her, as she cooked his meals and washed his clothes. She had tried to get him out and to make new friends and try new activities, but he just wasn't interested. He felt he didn't need to – he had all he needed whilst living with his daughter and grandsons.

Laura appeared to be keeping her life on hold for him, just in case. Her father might need more support in the future but, at the moment, he was still independent. Laura had put her caring duties high up her priority list, despite them not being needed at that moment. She was so used to putting others before herself that it had become a habit. As a result, Laura had prevented herself from realising her full potential as a qualified counsellor.

I asked Laura if she thought she might be too caring and

whether she and her father had become co-dependent on one another. I suggested that Laura needed to provide for herself and her children. As and when her father eventually died, what would happen to her future? What of her chosen career? Wouldn't she rather be earning whilst doing something she loved – counselling – rather than perhaps working in a dead-end job to make sure the bills were paid? As much as she loved her father, she deserved to live her own life and pursue the career of her dreams.

I explained to Laura that her life was happening right now and her dreams should not be put off. This time would never come again and building her own life was a key priority.

Being too selfless can have a negative impact on both you and your loved one

It can feel uncomfortable doing something you don't usually do. Many carers are so used to putting others first, it can then feel awkward to focus on themselves. Their instinct is usually to keep giving. In contrast, the cared-for may become so used to this attention, that they could turn inwards. Their world becomes just about them and their needs, forgetting the needs of others or to ask how they are. One carer would remind her husband, who had been ill for many years, that when his friends called him to see how he was, he needed to also ask how *they* were.

So over-caring can have a negative impact on both parties. When Neal was still able to stand and walk, despite being somewhat wobbly, I could have persuaded him to do more, even if it was under my guidance. However, because he was so used to me buzzing around him, bringing food and cups of tea to the sofa whilst he sat watching TV, he came to expect it. Who wouldn't? If it were me, I imagine I would do the same. In over-caring for Neal, and bringing everything he needed to him, this stopped him from exercising his legs, using his hand-to-eye coordination and taking a break from sitting for the majority of the day.

If I did something all the time, he came to expect it. It wasn't anybody's fault. We were just unaware of the pattern of behaviour we had fallen into.

If your loved one can stand and walk, even for a short while, it is good for them. Standing raises the heartbeat, which in turn burns calories. Weight bearing is so important for strengthening the legs, and helps to keep us active for longer. It's a shame I wasn't aware of this, because, as Neal's mobility waned, we relied more and more on the wheelchair and transferring him into it became increasingly difficult.

I know it can be quicker and easier to finish a chore, rather than let your loved one do it, but in the long run you may be making a rod not just for your own back, but also for theirs. You may have heard the saying, 'killing with kindness'?

Empowering your loved one will help to empower you

When I realised that sitting for long periods of time was not doing Neal any good, I had an idea. It was a Friday afternoon, and as Neal sat on the sofa watching his usual TV programmes, a lovely woman called Brenda from a befriending charity came to sit with him for the afternoon. This was a weekly visit, and whilst she spent a few hours with Neal, I would head off and do something for myself. It was also good for Neal to see another face instead of mine all of the time.

This particular afternoon, before I headed off, I spoke to Brenda on the quiet and asked her if, instead of her making him a cuppa, she would ask him to make one for her. She smiled wrily and agreed to try as I headed out of the door for a few hours.

Later, when I returned, I was in the kitchen, and Brenda came to join me.

'Did you manage to get him to make you a cup of tea?' I asked.

She laughed. 'Well yes, he did, but he wasn't too happy about it.'

We both chuckled because we knew what Neal was like. Brenda continued, 'He got himself up off the sofa and I walked with him into the kitchen. He boiled the kettle and, as he reached for the cups and poured water into them with a bit of a face on him, I asked, "Are you making it with love, Neal?"'

Brenda and I did laugh. I knew he wouldn't appreciate being asked to do something, because others always did everything for him. It was outside his usual pattern of behaviour. The simple exercise of making a cup of tea did Neal good, even if he wasn't impressed. Standing and walking to the kitchen would have raised his heartbeat and making the tea would have caused him to use his hand-to-eye coordination. He would have also exercised his waning balance. Making a cuppa doesn't sound like much, but for someone whose physical health was in decline, it helped to exercise both his brain and his body.

If you are the one doing all the chores, even though your loved one could help, this co-dependency may become routine. It then becomes more difficult to get them to help you around the house or do things for themselves. They may even think, 'Why should I, if I have you, my carer?'

If the cared-for is able to do some things for themselves, but you still do everything, you could find yourself swamped in a never-ending to-do list. You then leave no time for yourself and, at the close of the day, you'll fall into bed exhausted. Some days I said to myself, 'I'll just do this,' and then, 'I'll just do that,' and by the end of the day I had run out of 'me time', and was left exhausted. All those small chores added up.

I know of some carers, who refuse help from others but then become resentful, feeling they *have* to do everything themselves. The elderly mother of a friend of mine moved in with her for a short while and, even though her mother was capable of helping around the house, and had even offered to do so, my friend wouldn't allow her mother to help. However, my friend then complained about her mother, saying she had to do everything. This was only true because she had made it that way.

If we do everything for our loved ones, even though there may be things they could do for themselves, we may feel put upon and eventually become exasperated. This may then leave the cared-for feeling disempowered and possibly even a burden.

A step too far

Carers often have to make many decisions for their loved ones. They can become highly experienced in caring, as they know their loved one intimately. In this situation, they then might think they know the mind of the cared-for, but making *all* the cared-for's choices for them can leave the cared-for feeling even more disempowered. For example, choosing what *you* think they would like to eat in a restaurant. My gran used to order for my granddad all the time. It actually became quite funny. Her usual quip was, 'He's having chicken.'

If you notice yourself making all the decisions for your loved one, try collaborating with them to ensure their opinion is at least considered.

Some carers can become so absorbed in their caring role that they find being indispensable, empowering. This reliance entrenches the carer's place in their loved one's life and provides them with a sense of security and importance. By showing how hard they work and how much they may have given up to care, the carer confirms their martyr's role.

And sometimes the cared-for can overstep the mark. I have known of long-term carers who have ended up with their own illnesses, and the cared-for had made it clear this was not appreciated – it was *they* who was ill and should receive the attention, not the carer! One woman, who had fallen ill with cancer whilst caring for her husband, told me how he had remarked one day, whilst she was receiving treatment, 'You and that bloody chemo!'

As she shared her story, we actually had a chuckle about it, but these remarks can be hurtful when you have given so much and are enduring your own health issues. If you notice this negative behaviour from the cared-for, try making them aware of how you feel and that you also need love and support. Also, confide in those who have love and compassion to help see you through.

Delegate!

If you are asked to do something, notice how you feel before agreeing. Do you have the time or energy to spare? Safeguarding your energy levels will help to stop you from becoming depleted.

If you can't do everything, don't feel inadequate or shy in accepting help. Try sharing the responsibility. Make a list of friends and family who could help out now and then. Some family members are more likely to help than others. Alternatively, some would love to help out but may feel awkward in asking, so you may have to suggest ways in which they could help. Then make a list of small tasks that anyone could easily take care of, like washing up, going to the shops or taking your loved one for an appointment. Whatever it might be, it will help to reduce the pressure on you. If others do come and help, make a point of letting them know how appreciative you are. They are then more likely to help you again. For example, do you have family members who are good at finances, or with DIY, who could help? Could you take advantage of this?

Although some people may offer to help, others when asked may refuse. Try not to take this personally. You never know – they may offer to help at a later date. And if someone does offer their support and helps a number of times, try not to ask them too often.

Over to you...

- Do you think you may be an empath? Do you feel others' pain and suffering easily? You can take an empath test online – go to www.empathtest.com to see how high you score. If you are easily drained by other people and situations, why not carve out time every day to give you space to focus on yourself?

- Are there chores you normally do that the cared-for could do for themself? If so, why not list them and discuss which they could do to help you? This might also empower them.

- Have you turned down help from others when it has been offered? If so, why? Others may not be able to do something as well as you can, but does that really matter? Understandably, you need to be able to trust someone with administering medication or hoisting, but there may be other tasks where they could help.

- Write a list of family members and friends who could help you. Also, jot down a list of the chores that they could help with. Then find an opportune moment to have a chat with them to see if they would be willing to help. If you don't ask, you will never know.

12

Caring the easier way

If you were to train for a marathon... 'Ugh!' I hear you cry, 'What, on top of everything else?'

Bear with me... If you knew you were to run 26 miles, you wouldn't just don your trainers, head off to the starting line and wait for the starting gun to go off. You would spend months in training, ready for the big race day. Not only that, you would need the right footwear and to take note of what to eat before, during and after the race. Plus, you would look at the way you run to make sure you didn't damage or hurt yourself during the months of training, ready for the long run.

I know this because I ran the London Marathon in 2014 to raise funds for The Brain Tumour Charity, which had supported Neal and me over many years. As hard as the hours of training and the run itself were, they weren't as hard as caring for a terminally ill husband for all those years. I would say running a marathon was easier and less painful, and it was over in a lot less time!

I jest, but it is true. Running all that way was actually easier than caring for my husband over all those years – and some people *die* running a marathon.

Whilst we all know you need planning, technique and organisation to complete a challenge or goal successfully – for example, painting a masterpiece, where thousands of hours are needed to perfect your brush strokes and mix the colours required – there appears to be little guidance or planning for caring for a loved one. You are pretty much left to it and often struggle at every turn.

And while creating a beautiful painting or finishing a race in record time are great achievements, I believe caring is much more important. It keeps loved ones safe and, possibly, alive for years longer. Sadly, the majority of people don't see how crucial caring actually is, and it is still greatly undervalued. Imagine a world where nobody cared?

As with learning new skills to master and achieve a goal successfully, caring can also make use of guidance and techniques to help you, not only to look after a loved one successfully, whilst safeguarding your own health, but to make your own life easier.

As I mentioned at the beginning, every carer's situation is different, depending on the nature of their role and what it entails. For example, if you are caring for a loved one, as well as holding down a job and bringing up a family, you are going to need good organisational and delegation skills, otherwise you will be exhausted in no time.

Being organised can alleviate unnecessary stress

If your loved one is bedbound, you will need to learn moving and handling techniques to ensure you don't hurt your back or your loved one when you turn or lift them. You may also need specialist equipment, like a hoist, and to undergo appropriate training to keep everyone involved safe. Carers often need to learn a whole set of new skills – more than most people imagine.

The following sections offer ideas on ways you can make your life easier when caring. I know because I discovered them, often at my own cost!

Manage your time

Most of us live hectic lives, but when a loved one falls ill, we have a whole new set of tasks on top of our usual ones. Your head can spin as you struggle to get everything done. If you feel you have too much to do, look at your tasks and decide which are negotiable and which non-negotiable. What do you really have to do and what is not so urgent? Are there tasks that can be left for now? Trying to do everything will leave you exhausted.

A good way to cope with a sea of chores is to write everything down. Use a notepad or, if you have a mobile phone, use the 'Notes', which I found useful. There are other apps like Evernote that help you to store lists of information. Dividing tasks between 'Urgent' and 'Non-Urgent' can help you manage your day.

No need to rush

If you are taking your cared-for for an appointment, allow plenty of time to get ready and out of the house, especially if your loved one has mobility issues. I found this out to my cost when I took Neal for a dental appointment. By the time I had transferred him into his wheelchair and then into the car and out again at the dental surgery, I knew we were a little late, but when we went in, the receptionist shook her head.

'You're too late. The dentist has taken in another patient.'

I was perplexed. I checked my watch. We were nearly 20 minutes late.

'Really?' I asked. 'Neal can't see the dentist?'

The answer was a resounding 'No', so we had to make another appointment and go through the whole routine again. Luckily, they did not charge me. I took Neal home but I had learnt my lesson. From then on, I allowed more time to get us both ready and out of the house. Instead of rushing and arriving late, it was more relaxing for both of us, to arrive early.

Value your time.
If you don't, no-one else will

Don't you hate rushing? Lacking organisation can put extra pressure on you. I have also made mistakes when rushing. I have ended up bumping or hurting myself and then getting more irate. Not a great way to be.

If you organise yourself, not only will you arrive punctually, but you will do so in a better frame of mind. It will be a more relaxed experience for both of you. Of course, you cannot anticipate everything, and if a loved one needs the toilet just as you are about to leave the house, or transport is late, there is not a lot you can do, but remain calm and deal with the challenges as they arise.

Two heads are better than one

If your loved one has been diagnosed with a condition or illness, there may be many questions you want to ask the doctor. Also, when dealing with your own illness, you can feel overwhelmed when discussing it with a specialist, so we always found that two heads were better than one. Before arriving at the hospital, we would discuss what was happening with Neal's health together, and write down any questions we wanted to ask. Then when we visited his healthcare specialist, I would also be present as I would often ask questions Neal hadn't thought of. This made the most of the time during those important consultations.

Whilst waiting for appointments at the hospital, I met patients who refused to let their family members join them when they went in to see their doctor. If the carer is left outside to wait, it can be difficult for them but we have to respect our loved one's wishes. It is their condition and their personal journey. We can give them our love and support, but it is for them to decide how they deal with their condition.

Neal and I frequently asked for a second opinion. Don't be afraid of doing so. It is always good to hear other specialists' views. Some second opinions proved fruitful, some less so. You may be pleasantly surprised and discover new treatments or ideas that can help. If you don't ask, you'll never know.

Contacts lists

There may be many telephone numbers to call, including doctors, hospitals, district nurses, and other specialists, to name but a few. Having all the contact numbers written down on one sheet of paper next to the phone or pinned to the refrigerator can save time sifting through a mountain of paperwork to find a number when you suddenly need it. I know it takes time to collate a contacts list, but once done, you do not have to think about it again. It is there at the ready. Our list was pinned to our fridge for years.

I also found that a medical list not only saved time but proved useful, especially if I was out and a doctor was called. If you create your own medical list for your loved one, information such as medication, next of kin, doctors' contact details, plus any other medical information that a healthcare professional might need in an emergency, will help. Also, letting others know that the list exists and leaving it in a safe place where anyone can find it, will help keep your loved one safer and reduce stress for all. My medical list for Neal was used often when paramedics were called. On arrival, when they needed to fill out their forms, I just handed it over and it saved me from having to repeat the details over and over again. Also, whenever Neal went into hospital, the list went with him.

Keeping yourself safe will help keep your loved one safe

Medical basics

A first aid course is a key piece of training for carers. Carers' centres and charities may provide these classes free, so do ask. Alternatively, speak to your doctor or other healthcare professionals, as they may point you in the direction of free first aid workshops.

Carers regularly take their loved one to the surgery or to hospital, which can be breeding grounds for bugs. So, wash your hands when you arrive, when you leave and when you return home.

Neal unfortunately came home with the antibiotic-resistant infection MRSA after being in hospital and, I then contracted it from touching him. We both then had to wash, head to toe, in an unpleasant pink goo every day and wait for three minutes for it to take effect and kill the bugs, before washing it off. I remember shivering in the shower and thinking that I wasn't overly impressed with this whole caring malarkey. Regularly washing your hands keeps you safer. If paid carers come into your home, ask them to wash their hands before they do anything, as they may have been caring for and touching another patient before visiting you.

Don't break your back!

It's a shame most carers are not informed how to look after their backs by learning moving and handling techniques. Caring for a loved one can be very physical and back problems are a common ailment. As I have mentioned previously, I had a bad back only two days after Neal came home from hospital and had become bedbound. After changing him late that evening, I headed upstairs to bed and it felt like there was a long sheet of toilet paper touching the whole of the back of one leg. I looked behind me to check, but there was nothing there. I groaned as I realised it was sciatica, stemming from my lower back. Over the following days, I ensured I strengthened my back with exercises. I then made sure I bent my knees whilst caring and didn't lean too far over, keeping my back straight and core tight.

When manoeuvring our loved ones, not only do we need to ensure our safety, but we also don't want to hurt them in the process. It can be easy to grab an arm to pull them up, but arms can be pulled out of sockets, especially if your loved one has become infirm. Neal often wore jogging bottoms, so one hand would grab hold of these and my other hand would be under his arm to help him up. Sometimes, I would click a handling belt around him, which gave me leverage to help him to stand up.

Carers' centres or other charities in your area often offer workshops on moving and handling. Once you have the knowledge, this will help to keep you safer and avoid injury. Just remember to keep your back straight and bend your knees. Also, don't try to overdo it – know your limits.

Wheelchair workouts

If you are using a manual wheelchair for your loved one, there are a number of techniques that can make life easier and safer. For example, when we first received the wheelchair from our local council, as I mentioned earlier, the chair had no seatbelt. I didn't realise how dangerous this was until Neal fell out of his wheelchair. There also weren't any handle brakes installed, so I asked for these to be added as Neal was nearly twice my weight and size. It would have been too dangerous to wheel him up and down slopes without them.

When brakes were installed on the handles, I felt more confident taking Neal out. One beautiful sunny day, I decided to push him down to the river at Richmond-upon-Thames. Down one side of the road was a steep slope leading directly to the towpath. I assumed I had more muscle than Superman and started to wheel him down. Within moments we picked up speed. I squeezed the wheelchair brakes hard, but because Neal was heavy, he and the wheelchair kept going; in fact, we speeded up. I was wearing shoes with no grip and, as I dug my feet into the pavement, I started to ski in them. Finally, I steered the wheelchair into a wall on our left. Neal's knees hit the bricks, luckily not too hard.

He called out, 'Ow!'

'Sorry, Neal,' I cried, 'but the alternative would have been a whole lot worse.'

I had met my limits manoeuvring him and I clearly needed different footwear too.

Footrests on a wheelchair are also very important. If your loved one's feet are left on the ground and you start to push, you can force their legs under the chair and cause injury.

Over the first few months of pushing Neal in his wheelchair, I came up against a number of issues. As we hadn't received any instruction, I was learning on the go. I happened to mention this at Richmond Carers' Centre one day. Their response was great. Together, we created a video that appears on YouTube, called *Using a Wheelchair - general tips*. It offers advice, including reversing the wheelchair down a slope or curb. The video also includes a great tip when pushing a wheelchair across gravel – don't push forwards, the small wheels at the front will buckle, but pull the wheelchair backwards, making it much, much easier. To view this video, go to YouTube and type in 'Using a wheelchair – general tips' or type/paste https://bit.ly/2UAkeCD into your web browser.

If your loved one is outside in their wheelchair for a long time, make sure they are warm enough. Even though we may keep warm by pushing them, they will be sat still for long periods of time and could get cold quickly. There is also special clothing for those sat in a wheelchair to keep them warm. Neal had what looked like a fake-fur-lined sleeping bag, with a waterproof outer layer – a wheelchair cosy – which his legs went into and pulled right up to his chest, keeping him warm when we were out on rugby days.

Even though Neal was big, I still thought I could walk at my usual speed whilst pushing him. So I would continue to walk fast, even though I was pushing a heavy husband. This led to me breathing heavily into his right ear. I soon became worn out and realised I not only needed to slow down, but also to change my technique. I had recently learnt a new running style, where you take smaller steps and slightly fall forwards. I decided to try this with pushing the wheelchair and it worked a treat. So if you find you run out of steam whilst pushing a loved one, try holding the wheelchair handles, taking smaller steps and leaning slightly forwards, relaxing into it. This technique propelled us both along with minimum effort and was much more comfortable and easy.

This technique came in very handy when we visited Florence with my parents. My father kindly took over pushing Neal in his wheelchair, but as Dad tried to walk at *his* usual fast pace, sweat dripped down his nose and Neal bounced around in his wheelchair like a rubber ball. I was hoping that the day out in Florence was going to be one of beauty and romance – it was neither. As Dad got hotter and more irate, I took over the reins to push Neal. Although my father was stronger than me, my technique needed less effort. I did try showing Dad, but he'd had enough by then. He clearly needed a beer!

Those long waits at the hospital...

Most carers have to endure long hours waiting with their loved one for appointments. I dread to think how many months of my life I have spent sitting in hospital waiting rooms with Neal. It was boring and draining.

In the end, I decided not to waste that time, so I took a bag of goodies – books, magazines, a flask of tea and something to eat. During our waits, Neal usually fell asleep in his wheelchair and I had something to occupy my time. It kept my mind active and I didn't get so frustrated with the delays. You can only stare at a wall for so long.

Communicate, however you can

As I have said, every so often Neal would go into our local hospice to give me a break. Because he was unable to speak, he couldn't let staff know if he needed anything. He was still rather partial to a packet of biscuits (one of his last pleasures in life). But when I returned to pick him up at the end of the week, the biscuits were untouched in his drawer, even though I had told the staff about them.

One week, when Neal was in the hospice, his friend, Paul, visited, and told me how he'd seen some of the staff moving and changing Neal in his bed. The staff had just talked over him, as if he was not there. I know Neal couldn't speak but he knew what was going on. This saddened me, so the next time Neal went in for respite care, I spoke to the staff and created posters to put up on the wall in his room. These posters asked staff if they would feed him his biscuits now and then. They also alerted staff that although he was unable to speak, he was still aware of his surroundings.

Hospitals and hospices have rotas and different staff will look after our loved ones at different times. Even if you speak to one member of staff, they will not always be on duty. Other staff will eventually relieve them. Ideally, all staff should look at patients' notes to make sure they know all details, but I found this didn't happen. Putting up posters around Neal's bed ensured staff were aware of Neal's needs, and this made his week more pleasant.

Toilet duty

Finding better ways of doing things will not only make your life easier, but may also be safer for your loved one. For example, if your loved one is bedbound, they can become constipated. Doctors usually prescribe laxatives and I would give these to Neal as and when needed. As both I and the paid carers would change Neal, separately and at different times, after he had emptied his bowels, we found that we could not keep track of when he had, or hadn't 'been'. I would ask the carers a day later if he'd had a bowel movement, but often they could not remember. As Neal could not speak, he could not let us know if he was constipated. In the end, our not knowing caused him severe pain and I realised I needed to take action to ensure this did not happen again. So, I drew up a list on an A4 sheet of paper and left the carers to fill in blank spaces. I would then know if Neal had 'been' and, if not, give him some laxatives. This worked reasonably well until I discovered some of the carers had illegible handwriting! In the end, I changed the form as shown in Table 1, so they just had to tick the boxes. This worked fine and the problem was solved.

Table 1: Chart for recording bowel movements and urine flow

Date	Time	Description *(wee or bowel movement)* Please tick
		Urine ☐ Big ☐ Medium ☐ Small ☐ **Bowel** ☐ Hard ☐ Soft ☐ Big ☐ Medium ☐ Small ☐
		Urine ☐ Big ☐ Medium ☐ Small ☐ **Bowel** ☐ Hard ☐ Soft ☐ Big ☐ Medium ☐ Small ☐
		Urine ☐ Big ☐ Medium ☐ Small ☐

Being organised not only helped alleviate Neal's unnecessary suffering, but it also gave me one less thing to worry about – so long as the carers filled in the form.

> *'For every minute organised, an hour is earned.'*
> Benjamin Franklin

Over to you...

- If you rush to get something done or to be somewhere, could you factor in more time? Do you notice how long something takes without rushing, like dressing your cared-for? You can then factor this time in when getting ready to go out, to save you from putting pressure on and exhausting yourself.

- If you find you are always rushing, make a concerted effort to relax and slow down during the day. Try taking time out between each chore. Then, notice how you feel that evening. Do you feel any the better for it?

- Do you struggle to remember all that you need to do? Could you make lists to prioritise tasks each day? Using a paper pad, tablet or mobile phone, you could organise your chores into urgent and less urgent. Writing down all that you need to do can help reduce the stress of trying to remember everything.

- If you take your loved one to the doctors' or hospital, do you have questions ready to ask the specialist to make sure you benefit as much as you can from the consultation? Why not have a conversation with your loved one before the appointment and discover what questions they would like to ask?

- Do you have a list of contacts with all the important telephone numbers, so you can refer to it at a moment's notice? Do you also have a medical list ready, in case paramedics or the doctor are called out when you are not there? The medical list should include your loved one's:

- o Full name
- o Home address
- o Phone number
- o Next of kin
- o Date of birth
- o Condition/illness and usual symptoms
- o Medication(s)
- o Doctor's name and address of the surgery
- o Hospital specialists' names and contact details, plus any other information that could prove useful to healthcare specialists treating your loved one.

- If you can, make copies of the list and pin it up, along with your contacts list, where it is easily accessible for paid carers and family members.

- Are there chores you find difficult? If so, can you find ways of improving them to make life easier for you? You may be surprised. As soon as you start looking for ways of making life easier, you may then start to find ways to improve other parts of your life whilst caring.

13

Making ends meet

Money worries can be a big issue for carers. Many of us have to give up work to care, which can drastically reduce our income and bank balance, leaving us even more anxious and frustrated.

Caring can be an expensive business

Benefits on offer from the State and local authorities can be meagre. Sadly, the State cannot pay for everyone's care, and most of us need more financial support than we receive. Too many carers fall ill whilst shouldering the financial burden of care. In the UK alone, it is estimated that carers save the economy £132 billion a year. That's an amazing amount of money, but not for those of us selflessly paying with our own time and health, whilst desperately seeking inadequate benefits.

Caring cannot only be costly, as we may have to give up work, but there may be other costs such as medication or adapting the home. I needed to organise wheelchair taxis to take Neal to hospital, but these were more costly than a regular cab, I assume due to the time needed to manoeuvre a disabled person in and out of the car. Neal loved going to Bushy Park, a 15-minute drive up the road, but the return trip was a whopping £50. It was far too expensive for us, so I didn't take Neal to his favourite park for a number of years. Eventually, in addition to Neal's benefits, we received a mobility car, so I could drive him places without paying the hiked up price of a wheelchair taxi. As soon as it was delivered, I took Neal straight to Bushy Park's Woodland Garden, the place he loved, which was wheelchair friendly – a simple pleasure we both really enjoyed together.

Many of us need to use paid carers to help us, often using our own finances. I dread to think how many thousands of pounds Neal and I spent on care agencies over the years. It was a lot and it worried me. Would we have enough to pay for it all? In the end, I found some great private carers by word of mouth. They were half the price of care agencies and this helped save money. If I had only known this sooner, we would have saved a huge amount. If you do use a care agency but are happy to manage the paid care yourself, search online for professional carers in your local area, or ask other carers or charities.

Benefits are beneficial, however small

Are you receiving the benefits you are entitled to? Many of us are not aware of what is available. Ask at your local carers' centre or contact your local council. In the UK, there is a benefit called the Carer's Allowance, which isn't a lot, but it all adds up. Neal was on Disability Living Allowance, which helped enormously, but it only went so far.

Some carers believe they do not deserve benefits and feel guilty claiming them. Benefits are there for a good reason, so make use of them as much as possible. A few years ago, we made friends with, Sean, a young man who also had a brain tumour. Although his walking had deteriorated and he could apply for a blue badge (a blue badge allows you to park for free in many places where you would normally be charged, and often disabled spaces are situated close to the main door of supermarkets, hospitals and shops), he didn't want to be branded disabled and refused to have one. Whenever his mother parked at the hospital, she ended up paying a lot of money whilst he was inside receiving treatment for the day. She was forever darting outside to insert more coins in the parking meter. It was an added worry for her, when they could have utilised a blue badge and free parking.

Putting the paperwork in place

Finances can be a huge challenge. Whilst caring, I ensured a Lasting Power of Attorney was in place whilst Neal was still able to speak and sign his name. This avoided a huge amount of stress and many problems that, on top of everything else, I would have encountered years later. A Lasting Power of Attorney (LPA) or Power of Attorney (POA) is a legal document by which a person appoints one or more people to make decisions on their behalf. There are different LPAs covering health and welfare or property and financial affairs. You can choose which you want. We chose a financial LPA, as I felt I knew Neal well enough to decide any health decisions for him as and when they arose. By ensuring the financial LPA was agreed and signed, I could continue managing our money and keep our finances going within the home. Without it, I would have struggled years later to pay or challenge bills in Neal's name. I would also have had issues organising our bank accounts when, years later, the bank put unexpected charges onto Neal's account so that it went into overdraft and occurred further charges. If I hadn't had the LPA in place, we would have been charged more. Unexpected financial issues can appear later down the line. The LPA enables you to deal with these, stress-free.

There is a charge for administering an LPA. In the UK, they are long and detailed and must be correct before submission to the Office of the Public Guardian at PO Box 16185, Birmingham, B2 2WH, to be registered. Your solicitor will prepare it for you, for a fee. I completed ours myself and then took it to our solicitor to give it the once-over before I sent it off.

Does the cared-for want or need a DNR?

Caring can be a minefield and there are things we really do not want to think about, but once taken care of, we can put them to one side and get on with our lives.

When Neal lost the power of speech, I was worried that we did not have a Do Not Resuscitate (DNR) form completed and signed. Even if you are extremely unwell and receiving palliative care, paramedics will still attempt to revive you if you become unconscious.

Not long after Neal's diagnosis he had made it clear that he wanted to be subject to DNR. At that time we didn't do anything about it, but when he became very poorly, I was acutely aware that he would want this even more. I asked him one more time and he put his thumb up for 'Yes'. I spoke to his doctor and together we completed the form. I made everyone aware of it and the form was kept within easy reach of anyone coming into the home. A copy of the DNR form was also put into Neal's bag when he visited the day centre, just in case.

This took the pressure off me to ensure the right thing would be done if anything were to happen to him.

Talking to a loved one about the DNR form is not always easy, but making the decision takes pressure off the carer. It's not for you to make all the decisions.

Where there's a will there's a way

As well as a DNR form, has your loved one made a will? Once this has been drawn up and signed, it can be another load off your mind. This then leaves you to focus on quality time with your loved one. Once Neal and I had drawn up our wills together, it was something we didn't have to think about. I know it can be emotionally draining to think of these things, but try to see them as just forms. Once they have been sorted, you don't have to think about them again.

As well as a regular will, you can also have a living will. This document allows the cared-for to make choices about their end-of-life medical care, in case they become unable to communicate their decisions. If your loved one chooses to have a living will, once agreed, this can also help take the pressure off of certain decisions you would have had to make for them in the future.

Managing your money

Some of us have limited resources, and not much money, especially if we have given up our career or a job to care. As well as this, some of us are better at saving and utilising our money than others. For example, if I haven't got the money for something, I won't buy it. Years ago, when it came to my learning to drive and getting a car, I waited until I had a full-time job and paid outright for a cheaper second-hand car. In comparison, at that time, my friend purchased a new car on credit, paying a high interest rate and struggling with money. Her car was lovely, but I preferred to live within my means instead of enduring the stress of running into debt.

I only make this point with the cars because we can easily exacerbate a situation by making choices that will not benefit us in the long run, such as how we take charge of our finances.

We can sometimes be frivolous with our money, which is fine now and then, but if it becomes a habit, our finances can rapidly dwindle.

A good way of saving is to manage your money better, and it can really pay off. Organising your money can help you stay on top of your bills.

No matter what your situation, everyone can benefit from making more of their money by doing the following:

- Take time to plan your budget;
- Keep track of your income and spending;
- Ensure you receive all the benefits you are entitled to;
- Shop around to make sure you always secure the best deal.

Shopping in charity shops can pay off. You would be surprised what you can find in these treasure troves. I have bought glassware, clothes and even music very cheaply whilst my spending gave to charity.

Food bills can prove costly, but there are good cookbooks available to help you eat well for less. Many of us eat a lot of ready-meals, which are not only expensive but full of unhealthy fats, sugar and salt. If you generally tuck into processed meals, you could try cutting down and prepare your own simple dinners. Then see how much you save each week.

Going out can be costly, but not everything need be expensive when it comes to socialising. Instead, you could meet at a friend's house, or invite them over, or else head to a park and enjoy a walk or picnic.

Most of us have far too much stuff. Apparently, most of us only use 80% of what we actually own. There are often clothes, unwanted gifts and many other things we may not have touched for years. Selling them can yield extra income. Websites like eBay or Gumtree help with this. If you struggle to upload your items to these websites, ask somebody to help you. Alternatively, you can put an advert in your local shop window or sell unwanted items at a car boot sale.

If you find you are still struggling with a lack of funds, ask your local carers' centre. It may hold finance workshops, and/or have an advisor to help get your finances in shape.

Look after the pennies and the pounds will look after themselves

I spoke to a male carer who was self-employed and had cared for his wife for over a decade. Due to his caring responsibilities and almost daily visits to hospital to see his wife, his business had suffered and finances were not great. He recognised he needed to invest in his future. He wanted to be there for his wife, but knew he also needed to be there for himself – because nobody else would be.

When I gave up full-time employment to care, I was lucky enough to work part-time as a freelancer, working from home. As well as earning some money, it kept my hand in and the grey matter working. Mind you, trying to keep both plates spinning could at times be stressful. I would then have to know where to push back and say 'no'.

Planning ahead and managing your money can reap benefits in the long run

Many carers, who have been there for their loved ones for years, and found their caring role come to an end, not only reel from this experience, but struggle to find a job or earn an income. I know this may sound grim, but it is good to think about yourself and ensure there is some sort of contingency plan if circumstances change. Keeping an eye out for an opportunity or an idea that may arise in the future, may help you become, or remain, financially stable. Staying in touch with good friends or business contacts could prove fruitful if you need help or work now, or later on. You may have heard the phrase, 'It's not what you know, but who you know'. Leveraging what we can, and helping each other out as much as possible, can help to bridge gaps and keep us afloat financially.

Over to you...

- If you are struggling with paying bills, why not sit down and go through your finances to see where you could make cuts? What do you really need and where do you think money is being wasted?

- Even if at the moment you are not struggling financially, it may still be sensible to see where money is being spent. It really does all add up and you don't know for how long you may be caring. Safeguarding your finances now can avoid stress in years to come.

- Have you checked to see what benefits you are entitled to? Don't be shy! Pick up the phone and ask at your carers' centre or local council. You can also look online.

- Do you have a Lasting Power of Attorney in place? You can ask your solicitor, your local carers' centre, or look online, for more information.

- If you need to, have you spoken to your loved one about the 'Do Not Resuscitate' form? It can feel awkward to discuss it, but once the choice has been made and the form signed off, neither of you has to think about it again.

- Has your loved one made a will? This can also be a sensitive issue, but once filed, it takes pressure off both of you.

- Are there charities offering befriending services in your area, or even day centres which offer you weekly respite care? This can provide time for you to recuperate or even work for a few hours each week.

- Why not draw up a list of friends and contacts who might be able to help you find employment in the future? Even old work colleagues who have moved onto other jobs might have useful contacts. It is good to remain in touch, just in case your circumstances change.

14

Your doctor doesn't know everything

Healthcare specialists, including doctors, nurses, physio-therapists and many others besides, do an amazing job, helping to save lives and keeping us well. I know that if Neal hadn't had the operation when he was first diagnosed with a brain tumour, his life would have ended not long afterwards. He was very lucky to receive the right treatment and the latest image-guided technology to remove the cancer, not only to keep him alive, but also to keep him well during the early days of his illness.

In contrast, Neal had been misdiagnosed for months by his GP before it was discovered that the problem was something serious. He even took himself off to hospital a few times because he felt so unwell. He must have felt really bad, but he was later discharged after further misdiagnoses. Even when he couldn't stand any more and I called an ambulance to take him to hospital, he was again discharged with two headache tablets. Although he had arrived at the hospital unable to stand, after he had been administered saline intravenously during his visit he had then felt better, so it was presumed all was well.

I, on the other hand, was shocked and questioned their decision. There was clearly something wrong, but the doctors had done their box-ticking exercises, the standard procedures in A&E, and had decided to let Neal go. However, if you have a large tumour in your brain, it's only a matter of hours before you are admitted again, or worse. Twenty-four hours later he was back in hospital, but this time I refused to allow Neal to be discharged until they had investigated further. That was when they finally scanned his brain and his tumour was diagnosed.

I am sharing this story because only we really know how we truly feel. If we are feeling mentally or physically unlike our normal self, we should insist that our symptoms are taken seriously. Doctors may see us locally, or at hospital, for only a few minutes, with many patients to tend to that day. So, it is up to us to make our voices heard and push to see specialists if we feel something is not right, as many of us are misdiagnosed every day.

Even though Neal was misdiagnosed at first, he finally received great treatment thanks to research, highly trained doctors and other healthcare specialists, but these people do not know everything. Nobody does.

After Neal's operation, he received chemotherapy every week. Whilst this continued for years, we also looked into alternative therapies to improve his health and longevity. Other patients in a similar condition would tell us of supplements and other holistic treatments they had found helpful or that had even improved their health, but when we asked Neal's doctors about these, they made it clear they knew very little or nothing at all about them. Neal's oncologist would only prescribe patented drugs.

His doctor prescribed chemotherapy, which often made Neal very poorly, so I headed to the health food shop to discover what might help boost his immune system. Neal's white blood cell count was declining due to the drugs and I also wanted to make him feel better as he was often sick straight after the treatment. So I purchased a large jar of antioxidants, which I pulled from my bag to show the oncologist at Neal's next hospital appointment. His response was abrupt: 'I hope you've kept the receipt?'

This surprised me. I had been told the antioxidants would help support Neal's immune system whilst taking chemotherapy. I complied with the doctor's suggestion and took the tablets back the next day. The oncologist knew what was best, right?

Moving forward to the present, and knowing what I know today, would I take the supplements back now? No, I wouldn't. I realised, over many years and visits to the hospital, that not once did any of the doctors treating Neal's illness discuss nutrition. They never mentioned how important a healthy diet would be to keep Neal's body as fit as possible in healing from the cancer. Neal's doctors focused exclusively on pharmacology and patented drugs. They were not prepared to explore supplements or holistic remedies – and I doubt they had time. Natural supplements found in health food shops had not been tried and tested like licensed medication, so it was up to Neal and me to decide whether to try these alternative remedies.

Through other avenues, away from the hospital, we came to learn of important discoveries – for example, that sugar promotes cancer growth. No doctor ever mentioned this during the 13 years that Neal was ill.

We learnt a great deal about health, diet and alternative therapies, which could help support and improve the body and mind, but we discovered these elsewhere, away from the hospital. For example, beetroot contains micronutrients that are beneficial for the brain – great for helping to heal brain cancer. After reading a book on one woman's road to recovery after being diagnosed with cancer twice, I had a reverse osmosis water filter installed in the kitchen, which removed all contaminants and impurities from tap water. I then bought a juicer, as I discovered that raw nutrients helped heal and alkalise the body, as due to the normal western diet, our bodies can become too acidic which can lead to illness.

Neal wasn't overly keen on my beetroot, broccoli and carrot juice and I don't blame him. He preferred a cup of tea and a biscuit – who wouldn't? I continued to make juice for us both, however, as I believed this helped to keep Neal as healthy as possible.

After meeting a lovely couple during a talk on micronutrients for the brain, we were told of an alternative specialist doctor in the States who checked for certain markers in the blood for people with brain tumours. We arranged an appointment with her over the phone, after which Neal was prescribed a whole host of supplements to improve his health.

Of course, I cannot prove whether any of this made a difference, but I believe it all added up and helped keep Neal alive for longer. However, there was one particular supplement that I believe really did make a difference.

An awakening

Years later, when Neal had become bedridden after his stroke, and was unable to speak, I stood over him and watched him lie motionless. He continually looked up and stared at the wall to his right above him. He did not appear to be engaging with life at all. It was gut wrenching to see him in this state. I felt we had come to the end of the line, but then a friend told me a story about a holistic doctor.

This alternative doctor had trained and worked as a conventional medical practitioner until he was diagnosed with a whole range of serious health issues himself, including a tumour on his head. Western medicine was not helping him, so he decided to put an advert in the back of a medical journal to seek help. The advice it evoked led him to complementary medicines that eventually healed him. He realised that there was much more available than patented drugs and began training in complementary medicine. He now offered this professionally.

I loved this story and booked an appointment for Neal to see him. After I had wheeled Neal into his consulting room, he asked to know everything about Neal and what had happened up to that point. I explained that Neal had played rugby for years and that during one particular game, his head had been stamped on by another player. Fourteen stitches later, Neal was discharged from hospital but some of his friends, and I, believed this might have been the catalyst for the brain tumour, along with overuse of a mobile phone.

I chatted with the alternative practitioner for quite some time whilst Neal sat slumped in his wheelchair. The holistic doctor then prescribed a supplement that was basically nothing more than condensed lambs' brains – clearly not for the vegans amongst us! I agreed to dissolve and give these tablets daily to Neal via his feeding tube.

Over the next few weeks, Neal did not appear any different. We had another appointment booked to see this holistic doctor five weeks later, but because it was expensive and there appeared to be no improvement in Neal, I cancelled it. However, in the sixth week I was in for a shock.

First thing every morning, I would come downstairs, enter Neal's bedroom and tunefully call out with great affection, 'Morning, chicken!' I would then pull the curtains back and give him a kiss. Neal would open his eyes, but nothing more. This particular morning, as I called out to him, he immediately swivelled his head around and, staring me straight in the eye, gruffly said, 'Don't call me chicken!'

I nearly fell over. It was as though Neal had come back from the dead. He hadn't spoken or been able to move his head around in months and months. I stood over him amazed, scrutinising his face and eyes as he stared right back at me with his big blue eyes, and said, 'Oh my God, Neal.'

He hadn't looked like this in a very long time. I continued, 'You look *really* alert. Do you feel alert?'

His reply was instant and vehement as he nodded. 'Yes!'

I was amazed. The only difference in anything Neal was taking at that time was the tablets the alternative practitioner had prescribed.

In taking just one supplement, it was as if he had woken up

There had clearly been a significant change in Neal. Something had healed in his brain and I could only put it down to the new supplement he was taking. I then learnt that it could take up to six weeks for a new supplement to start working and it had taken exactly that. It was wonderful to be able to converse with Neal and I rebooked another appointment to see the holistic doctor. In those moments, I realised we should never give up hope because you just never know what else is available that could help to improve our health.

Although Neal was clearly better after taking this supplement, he was still in decline, and this wonderful improvement started to wear off after about a year.

We are lucky to have so much information at our fingertips via the internet. So many great books have been written and documentaries created by others who have been through similar situations that could help many more of us. We just need to look. Every day, there are many discoveries of countless amazing health alternatives and natural remedies. And unlike patented expensive drugs, which have many side effects, natural supplements are often much kinder to the body. *But I do want to be very clear, some supplements may interfere with medication, so do ensure you consult with your doctor first.*

Over to you...

- If your loved one has an illness or chronic disorder, have you looked into alternative therapies that could help them, even whilst they continue to take their prescribed medication? Some of us are more open than others to alternative medicines and not all loved ones are up for taking them. We can only research and suggest, but it is up to the cared-for to decide if they want to try them. We must always respect their wishes.

- If you socialise with others who are dealing with the same disorder, have you asked them if they have found any complementary or holistic medicines that have helped improve their loved one's health? Have they changed their diet in any way and noticed any improvements?

- There are many books on specific conditions on the market. Have you read any that could possibly benefit your loved one?

SECTION 3

Your support network

15

Taps and drains

When we are going through a huge life challenge such as caring, we need good friends and family, as well as local services and charities, around us to help. Our support network is key.

It is important to have the right calibre of friends and family supporting us. Some may not be as understanding or compassionate as others and it is important to recognise this. Often in times of challenge you get to see the best of people, but unfortunately you may also see the worst. Not all of us can cope well with illness or stressful situations.

Whilst I was caring, most family and friends were really there for me. They were supportive and picked me up when I was down. Sadly, that was not the case for all. As mentioned earlier in the book, there were some who knew I was struggling, but still managed to cause me further grief.

I would describe caring for Neal as being like living with two buckets of sand around my neck. The responsibility weighed me down and I already had enough to cope with, so, as you may imagine, it did not take much to topple me over.

After falling ill a second time from the stress of caring, Neal had ended up in a nursing home whilst I recovered. I realised that I had allowed others' poor behaviour and lack of support to contribute to my falling ill. I decided to share these thoughts with my good friend, Jo, one day whilst she had come to visit to see how I was. I spoke of two people in particular who had caused me a lot of grief. She then told me a fascinating analogy. People are either 'taps' or 'drains'. Taps are loving and giving, whilst drains, well, they are draining – usually of our time, our energy and even our happiness.

In that moment I had instant clarity. The penny dropped. It suddenly dawned on me that these few people I was having constant issues with were 'drains'. I even burst out laughing at this realisation. I had been expecting these 'drains' to be like me – caring and considerate. They were not and they were never going to be. I also noticed that all the 'drains' in my life had something in common – they all had a lot of their own personal issues and displayed little or no love or compassion. They struggled to offer support to someone in my position.

This new analogy opened something up for me. Shortly after Jo left, I took a piece of paper and sat at the table. At the top of the page, I wrote two headings - 'Taps' and 'Drains' - and drew a line between them, down the page. I thought of all the friends and family members in my life and quickly wrote their names under either one or other of these headings. Doing this quickly didn't allow me time to chew the cud over certain people – maybe they were a bit of both. I decided in a heartbeat which one they predominantly were.

After I had drawn up the two lists, I sat back to view the results. My list of 'Taps' was very long and extensive. Although my lists of 'Drains' was short, I was still surprised at some of those who appeared in this category. Even so, I smiled and told myself, 'Look at all the taps you have in your life. Focus on and surround yourself with them. Forget about the drains!'

I realised I had spent too much time focusing my energy on family and friends who were draining, and who had caused me upset and anguish. The sad fact was, that I had not been focusing on the more important list – the 'taps' – those good friends and family members who were there for me and were loving and giving. Why do we do this to ourselves?

Not everyone around you will have compassion

If someone upsets us, we often find this drama something we can chew on. We can spend a lot of time mulling it over, even if we have been enjoying time with the 'taps' in our lives. Unfortunately, the more we focus on something, the bigger it becomes. If you notice negative thoughts arising because of others' unpleasant behaviour, it would be best to move your attention away and onto those who are more loving and giving.

Most carers struggle with relationships at times, because the dynamics within the family can change when a loved one becomes unwell. Some friends and family have an amazing amount of empathy, but, conversely, some have little or none – even if they are members of your immediate family.

As well as categorising friends and family as 'taps' or 'drains', to ensure you surround yourself with the right calibre of folk whilst continuing to care, you could also ask yourself if they have empathy for your current situation. Working through the people in your life, you could also sort them under the categories of 'Empathy' or 'No empathy'. For example, my mother would go straight into the 'Empathy' category as she is always loving and supportive, whereas my previous HR manager would most definitely head towards 'No empathy'! It almost seems funny, but in becoming more aware of how people treat us and our situations, we start to realise how much, or how little, understanding they have. This can help us direct our communication towards those who are more likely to help when we are in need of more support.

Previously, I had made the mistake of assuming everyone else was like me. I had thought they saw the world as I did and had love and compassion. Many did not, and the same will apply to those around you. You will have loving and giving 'taps' in your life, but you will have 'drains' as well. We are all different. Some of us just happen to have more empathy than others.

If you decide to create your own 'taps and drains' list, you may conclude that some people are a bit of both. Sometimes they are a 'tap' but at other times a 'drain'. I have a few friends and family members like this. Most of the time, I see them as 'taps', but they can still cause me problems now and then. If and when this happens, I try not to take it personally and speak to them honestly about how they make me feel. If they continue to cause me grief, I keep them at arm's length until the issue has dissolved.

A few years ago, I gave a talk at an event for The Brain Tumour Charity in London. I spoke of the 'taps and drains' analogy. In the interval, a woman who cared for her husband came to speak to me. She liked my analogy and had a similar idea she had used when others around her were not supportive. She called it the 'cull'. Although I chuckled at the time, I found this label a bit strong as well as negative. She told me how some friends and family had been unkind and let her down, whilst she continued to care for her terminally ill husband. She just didn't have the time and energy to deal with those who clearly did not have her or her husband's best interests at heart during those difficult days. She felt she needed to cut them out of her life as she couldn't cope with them on top of caring. Some carers may feel this is a bit harsh but for others it may be the only way to safeguard their health and wellbeing.

I suspect that every family has at least one member who can be a bit of a drain. In fact, I think it's compulsory! Although some people in our lives may be draining, you don't have to do the full cull of everyone. I'm certainly not keen on falling out with family as this could fuel further stress in an already difficult situation. So instead, I keep my distance from any draining family members and only see them occasionally.

Some of us may live with somebody draining. If this is you, just try emotionally keeping your distance from them and don't take their behaviour personally. Often another's unpleasantness and unkindness are the result of what is going on inside them and how they are reacting to their own personal challenges. Their negativity may not have anything to do with you.

When I was on a silent retreat, I heard some wonderful advice from a 70-year-old ex-nun: if you run into a conflict with another, rather than *reacting*, use *creative engagement*. She said it was easy to fire back at another when that person pushed our buttons. This is how 'drains' usually behave. Reacting negatively to another, whether it is your fault or not, fair or not, usually only fuels a conflict. Someone has to offer peace and love to overcome the tension, otherwise it can escalate, draining us further.

Surround yourself with those who are there for you

If you surround yourself with the 'taps' in your life – loving and positive people – they will help keep you supported and, I guarantee, will help to improve your life.

Who or what is draining you?

Another great term for those who drain us is 'energy vampires.' I love this term as it exactly describes what these people do to us.

Whenever Neal and I headed back to see my family for a weekend, we always visited my elderly grandparents. They

135

weren't the most sensitive of souls and would often comment on Neal's appearance whilst he was having treatment for his cancer. They would say, 'Ooh, you've lost some hair.' Neal was also on steroids, which can make you gain weight. Even though they knew he was ill, they would still comment, 'Ooh, you've put on some weight.'

Elderly people can sometimes lose their inhibitions, and speak without thinking. Neal endured these comments without saying anything to me, until we were next to visit my grandparents. He asked me if I would mind going without him, because of their insensitive remarks about his appearance. I fully understood and told him that he didn't have to go again if he didn't want to. I know my grandparents' comments were not said with malicious intent, but they still hurt Neal and he had more than enough on his plate.

People, places or even situations can drain us of energy. There were times when I had agreed to be somewhere to support others, only to find it was not only a waste of my energy, but there was clearly no gratitude for my help. I quickly learnt not to allow these particular energy vampires to use up my resources again.

Over the years, Neal and I received love and support from people we wouldn't even have expected it from. I remember receiving kindness and understanding from complete strangers in hospital whilst Neal waited for treatment. There is always someone wanting to give their love.

When I sat in a local café with a friend, discussing how I was raising money for The Brain Tumour Charity, by running a marathon, out of the blue, a stranger leaned over and gave me £100 towards the fundraising. When these special moments happen, they can remain with us for years.

The drama triangle

As I mentioned, when a loved one falls ill, this can alter the dynamics within the family. If you are the one doing all or most of the caring, you may at times feel burdened and even unappreciated. The judgements of others can rob us of self-worth, especially if we are sensitive and easily hurt. People will always judge, but it's up to us how we take this on board.

There is a great model that can help to clarify behaviour when conflict arises. The 'drama triangle' was created in 1968 by Dr Stephen B. Karpman MD* and it involves three different role types – the Persecutor, the Rescuer and the Victim.

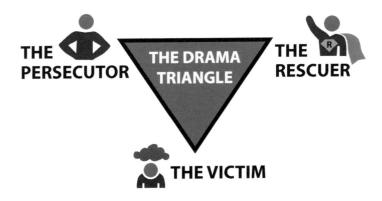

Understanding how these three roles interact, can help us resolve difficult conflicts and relationships, which may drain our energy.

* Footnote:
Karpman, S. (2014). *A Game Free Life: The New Transactional Analysis of Intimacy, Openness, and Happiness.* San Francisco: Drama Triangle Publications.
Karpman, S. (2019). *Collected Papers In Transactional Analysis.* San Francisco: Drama Triangle Publications

The Rescuer takes responsibility for other people's problems and tries to solve them. In the process, they often disregard their own issues, in order to take care of everyone else's.

The Victim feels helpless and powerless in the face of what is happening around them. They think, 'Why me?'

The Persecutor is often frustrated and self-righteous. They tend to blame others and tell them how they, the Persecutor, believe they are always right.

We can move between these roles, depending on the situation, but most of us predominantly play one of them and are defined accordingly. If you are experiencing a conflict, being aware of these roles can help you decide where you are in the triangle and empower you to resolve the issue.

If you are feeling helpless and overwhelmed, you may be in the **Victim** role. If so, try becoming a survivor and problem solver. Decide what you want and what steps you need to take to get there. What can you take control of? Also, reflect on what is going right in your life or what you are grateful for – even if it is only the hot shower you had that morning. This will help improve your state of mind.

If you think you are usually in the **Rescuer** role, it would help to support and encourage others to solve *their* problems rather than striding in to fix it for them yourself. Ask others what they think they may need to do to improve their situation. Make sure you set boundaries for the amount of time you spend helping them. Remember, if you are caring for someone already, you have enough on your plate without taking on more responsibilities. You can't save everybody.

Finally, if you often think you may be in the **Persecutor** role, becoming frustrated with others, try listening to them instead of blaming them. There are two sides to every story. Be diplomatic in your approach and make others aware of where you are coming from, whilst setting boundaries. For example, if you make an agreement with them, suggest that, if you keep your side of it, you expect them to stick to theirs. Make it clear that a particular issue may not be your problem to solve.

As carers, we often have to deal with conflicts arising from our stressful situation; becoming aware of our own behaviour enables us to identify which role we are playing and to change tactics to ensure a better outcome for all. Remember, creative engagement, not reaction.

I was very much the Rescuer whilst I was caring, desperately trying to ensure everyone else was happy, even though I was often depleted. In the end, I had to take a step back and ensure my own wellbeing.

In his book, *The Four Agreements* (1997), Don Miguel Ruiz advocates one particular 'agreement': 'Don't take anything personally'. I know this can sometimes be difficult, but we may not know how another is feeling or thinking. As I have said, often their unpleasantness and lack of kindness involves what is going on inside *them*. Their negativity may not have anything to do with you, and they may be struggling with the situation.

There will always be people in our lives who either fill us up or drain us. We are all so different. Dr Wayne Dyer was an American self-help author and a motivational speaker, and he used the metaphor of an orange to explain this difference. If you were to squeeze an orange, what would come out? A simple enough question. If you were to squeeze the orange many times over, apple juice would never come out. If you keep squeezing, you won't get grapefruit juice to come out of it either. The only thing that will ever come out of an orange, as you know, is orange juice.

Although simplistic, the question is, 'why?' Why does orange juice only ever come out of an orange? It's because that's what's inside it, and so however hard you squeeze the orange, that is what will always come out.

Now extend this metaphor to someone you know, who you may be having a difficult time with. If they are squeezed and put under duress, what comes out of them? It could be emotions such as frustration or possibly anger. If they then project this negativity in your direction, and say something to you that you don't like, or if they behave in a way which you find offensive, they may hurt your feelings. *You* will then become 'squeezed'. At that point, what emotions will come out of you? Would they be negative or display love and understanding?

Whichever emotion comes out of you, this is what was inside of you. You may be thinking that this person hurt you, even whilst you were doing your best. The fact is, people do things to you all the time on the outside, but you live your life on the inside, with your thoughts and feelings. We cannot control others' behaviour, but we can control what we think and how to react. This is what will make the difference between being a fully functioning person or maybe playing the victim.

When something bad happens to you, you either learn from it or allow yourself to be trampled by it. Dr Wayne Dyer wrote that there are no accidents in a perfect universe, only lessons. *Everything that happens is a lesson.* So the next time a conflict arises in your life, what are you learning?

He also remarked that you cannot give away what you don't have. For example, if you wanted a dozen oranges, I wouldn't be able to give you those oranges unless I went out and bought them. The same applies with those who don't have any love within them. They can't give love to others if they don't firstly have the love inside themselves to give away. If you only have contempt, anger or fear inside you, then these will be the things you dish out to others. What comes out of us, is what is inside.

Over to you…

- Who do you feel is there for you and who drains you? Why not make your own list of 'taps and drains' to clarify who is really there for you, and who drains you, so you know who to keep at a distance, either emotionally or physically?

- What values do you see in the people in your life who are 'taps'?

- Which 'taps' will you be hanging out with this week? And how do they make you feel when you have been with them?

- Are there any places that make you feel drained? Sometimes, waiting in hospitals can be draining, or visits to certain friends or family members. If you notice these are draining you, try avoiding being in these situations.

- Have you ever been surprised by an unexpected gift or kindness from someone? Have people given you helpful information when they have found out you are a carer? We can easily latch on to the negative remarks of others, but it is essential to remember those who have given us time, love and gifts, especially when we have least expected it.

- Finally, which of the three roles do you usually see yourself play within the Drama Triangle? When you have been in a conflict, which roles did you see the other people play? How could you make changes to help smooth out any issues you have with them? This would benefit not only you, but everyone around you.

16

Should they care?

Something many carers notice is that if you are the one stepping up to help, you can almost guarantee some other family members will take a step back, or leave you to it altogether.

A few doors down from where I live, a man in his 50s, who lives alone, looks after his mother who lives across the road. He has organised for paid carers to go in and help whilst he is at work, and then he is supporting her in the evenings and at weekends. Meanwhile, his sister, who has her own family, has moved away. One day, as I was standing in my driveway, he came over and complained at the lack of support he received from his sister. I smiled and said, 'Welcome to the club!'

I told him most carers have to deal with this issue. However, if you are the one doing most of the caring, shouldn't you expect other family members to do their bit? If you have family who fall short of helping you, there may be a number of reasons for this:

- They are living a hectic life, juggling work and family, with little time for anything else, including helping you
- Work dominates their lives and is their priority
- They don't understand what you are going through
- They feel awkward around someone who is ill, or needing help, and so stay away

- They don't want to get involved or have the responsibility, so they hope that you will take over.

When others avoid us or refuse to help, we can feel betrayed. It can lead to feelings of frustration and anger, especially when we are giving so much whilst others may give so little. It can be very easy to fall out over this, and I know of families who have. If you are trying to get a family member to help, you could try asking them to come and give assistance for just a few hours at first. For example, you could tell them you need to be somewhere for an afternoon or an evening, and could they come and be with the cared-for whilst you are out? Let them know how appreciative you would be. Your gratitude may persuade or inspire them to help you more.

If you think a family member is keeping their distance because they feel awkward or even scared of what is happening, try talking to them and rationalise the position. We all fall ill and we need to be there for each other. Also, the loved one may only be here for a limited amount of time, so making the most of the care together will make these days easier to bear and create fond and loving memories. These days, weeks and months will not be back.

Obviously, you can try communicating with family and asking for help, but they may still refuse. I worked with a woman named Tracy at a local charity, who cared for her mother after she had had a stroke and become frail. Tracy lived over 200 miles away from her mother whilst holding down a busy career job. Every weekend she would drive the distance to take care of her mother. When I asked Tracy whether there were other family members who lived closer to help her mother, and save her from the long drive every weekend, she told me she had a brother. He lived only a few miles down the road from her mother but he rarely visited.

'Could you not ask him to help more, as it is getting too much for you?' I asked.

She shook her head. She had tried many times but had now given up asking because it had become too stressful. She would rather get on with the caring herself to ensure her mother was well looked after.

We can ask others for help, but to keep asking and being rejected can add another layer of stress. Sometimes we just have to let go of those who will not help, and this could then even feel like a weight lifted.

Letting go of those who refuse to help can often be a weight lifted

Even if family refuse to help, as difficult as it can be, try not to burn relationship bridges. If someone is causing you a lot of grief, try to keep your distance and emotionally let them go. If they are hurtful, recognise it's their issue, not yours. We are simply not all as understanding as we could be.

Absent friends

Neal loved his rugby and I would often take him in his wheelchair to see a match, which was a 10-minute walk down the road. After the match, as he tired easily, I would take him straight home, hoist him into bed to rest and leave a paid carer with him for a few hours. I would then head back to the stadium to have a few drinks and catch up with friends whilst Neal slept.

As I strolled back to the stadium one evening, leaving Neal tucked up under the watchful eye of a carer, I got a call from one of our friends back at the bar. He told me one of Neal's longest and closest friends, Gary, who lived over 100 miles away, had been right there in the grounds chatting with him and had just left to go home. Neal had not seen this friend in five years.

'You're kidding me?' I remarked astonished, 'Gary was there with you just now?' As our house was only a short walk away, Gary could easily have popped his head in and seen Neal for a few moments before heading home. He had probably even passed our front door on his way to the stadium. Instead, even though Gary knew his sick and dying friend lived minutes away, he had chosen to leave without seeing him.

I hit the roof! I couldn't help it. How much effort would it have taken for him to see Neal, whom he had not seen for years? I was so disappointed, mainly for Neal, as many of his friends hadn't come to see him in years.

The following morning, as I was getting Neal up with the help of Sam, one of the paid carers, I asked for her opinion about Neal's friend's absence, as it was still troubling me. Sam was quite direct in her answer: 'Well, I'd tell him,' she replied. 'He needs to know'.

Perplexed, I replied, 'I know but I can't *force* him to come. I know it's not exactly a barrel of laughs sitting with Neal, who can't even speak nowadays. I know Gary came up for the rugby to have a good time with friends.'

'Well, I'd still tell him,' she insisted.

The thought of this conflict made me feel uneasy. 'Maybe I'll text him,' I said to her. 'At least he'll be aware that we were at the rugby as well. He will know for next time and we could then catch up.'

So that's what I did. My text read: 'Hi Gary, I hear you were at the rugby yesterday. Neal and I were there too. Let us know if you're here again. We would love to see you. Sara & Neal xx'

I pressed 'Send'. Not even 30 seconds had passed on that Sunday morning, before my mobile started to ring. Gary's name flashed up on my screen.

'Oh my God, he's calling,' I exclaimed. Although we had not spoken in five years, my text had taken seconds for the silence to be over. I cheekily answered, 'Hello, blast from the past!'

'Don't make me feel any more guilty than I already do,' he moped. We then had a good conversation and I told him how things were with Neal and invited him for a weekend. I suggested we took Neal out in the day, as this was Neal's best time, and once he was back in bed, we could have a night out to catch up over a beer. He agreed it was a good idea.

Sometimes it is down to us to initiate contact if we want to see friends

Initiating the contact myself, rather than waiting for Gary to call, helped bridge a gap that had existed for years. We all like to think our friends will be there for us, even in our darkest days, but sadly this is not always the case. They may find it difficult to visit if a friend is long-term sick, but even so, they are still their friend.

Once a loved one has fallen ill, many carers have found that they have never seen some of their friends again, even though they had been really close. Shocking isn't it? I tried reaching out to some absent friends by inviting them over but, once Neal had become disabled, it was as though they had disappeared. They did not even call or ask if he was still alive. I felt hurt and angry for a long time, but these negative emotions did not serve me. They actually made me feel worse. Eventually, I came to accept that they were gone. When times are hard, you really get to know who your friends are.

If you are noticing that friends seem to be drifting away and you want them to pay a visit, be positive and tell them how you would love to see them. You could even offer ideas on possibly meeting somewhere for a walk or a coffee. Of course, getting the diary out and agreeing on a date during the conversation will certainly make the visit or meet-up more definite.

When I first met Neal, he had so many friends. I don't think I knew anyone with so many. When he fell ill, most of them rallied around, filling up his hospital bedroom and enjoying the banter. One day, so many of his friends arrived at the hospital, that some were even turned away by staff.

During Neal's years of illness, his large circle of friends greatly reduced, which was hard for us both to accept, though several good friends remained and will always be very special. We discovered friends Neal had known for decades stopped phoning or coming to see him. In the first few years, I would take him out and about so he could see his friends, but as time went on and his mobility deteriorated, I could not take him very far. It really was down to his able-bodied mates to come to him. Sadly, many did not.

A good friend made a poignant comment. She said Neal had been ill for too long. I think she was right. By this time, he had been poorly for over a decade. The old Neal, full of fun, cheeky and great at getting people together, had become a shadow of his former self. Some friends would have found this hard to bear. I recall one friend who visited us one afternoon, admitted he'd cried on the train on his way home after seeing how bad his friend had become.

I discovered that some of Neal's friends, who had kept their distance, would ask on the grapevine to see how he was. I bumped into one of his previously good friends, Ken, whilst, again, at the rugby. He started to explain why he had not visited. He said that the days had turned into weeks, and the weeks into months, and now it had been years since he had last seen Neal. So, he had finally cut his losses. Those were his actual words, but at least he was honest. It was a shame, as I knew Neal would have enjoyed seeing Ken and hearing him talk of the old times whilst giving his latest news. Luckily for us, some friends still plucked up courage to visit and we really appreciated their effort.

So, back to the story of Gary at the rugby ground. After our phone call and agreeing to meet up, did he finally come and see his dear friend to spend time with him? Sadly, not. We can ask friends to visit us, but we cannot *force* them. It is their choice and one we have to accept. After this, I emotionally let go of Gary and rarely even thought of him, unless I looked at Neal's old photographs with his mates. There were a number of friends I finally regarded as history. This was not so much negative, but a way of coping. It gave me space and energy to focus on the good friends who were still in our lives. If those absent friends had suddenly appeared at our front door again, I would have welcomed them with open arms, but the important thing was to enjoy the family and friends who *were* there for us through those difficult years.

Cherish your special friends. I do not know what I would have done without mine. They kept me sane.

Over to you...

- We often expect family and friends to call if we are struggling, but could you try picking up the phone or emailing someone to revive communication? You could invite them over for a visit or to meet up somewhere? At least you will have given it one last shot.

- Finally, focus on the good friends and family who are there for you, and let them know how special they are.

17

A voice of reason

Carers have to make decisions for their loved ones every day, such as deciding the best treatment, organising their physical and emotional support, or maybe even choosing a nursing home. We want to make sure we make the right decisions, but sometimes these can be difficult and can even keep us awake at night.

If we struggle with a dilemma, it's good to have a voice of reason. A voice of reason is somebody you know and trust who will give you an honest opinion about anything you ask, and will guide you to the right solution. A voice of reason will not just have empathy, but insight and understanding of your current situation. They will not be influenced in their advice by personal gain and they will always have your best interests at heart. They are a sounding board upon which you can rely.

I was lucky to have two people whom I regarded as my voices of reason. One was Julia, a nurse from our local hospice, where Neal went for day care. One day, I called her with a dilemma.

Family members wanted Neal to travel over 100 miles to a wedding for a weekend. Since suffering his stroke, Neal had not been far from the house. He was mostly bedbound and could only sit in his wheelchair for a few hours a day. The family knew this but still kept on at me, saying how much they wanted him at the wedding. One even suggested Neal could stay in one of their homes. I was perplexed, because they knew we needed a hoist and a pressure mattress, of which they had neither. I would have loved him to be at the wedding too, but knowing how poorly he was, I thought, 'How on earth am I going to even get him all the way down there?'

Organising the journey and the weekend would be a lot of hard work, most of which would be down to me. Also, Neal would not fare well on such a long drive, and after all that, he might only be at the wedding for an hour or two at best. I would have to try booking him into a local hospice, which would have the necessary specialist equipment we needed.

This dilemma played on my mind for weeks as the wedding drew near and family kept insisting he come. It stressed me, so I decided to call Julia at the hospice and ask for her advice. Her reply was immediate: 'Is it in Neal's best interest?'

Her quick response surprised me and I laughed, 'No!'

I immediately felt better. Julia then shared the story of a similar situation, where someone as poorly as Neal had travelled the same kind of distance to the hospice. Like Neal, this other patient was also in palliative care, and they had had to hire an ambulance at a cost of nearly £2000.

'Whoa!' I exclaimed. 'There is no way the family will pay that kind of money and I don't see why we should, especially not even knowing how Neal would fare at the end of such a long journey.'

So, I relayed this conversation and cost to the family. Giving them the answer direct from a specialist nurse took the pressure off me. Instead, I suggested that, a few weeks before the wedding, the family could come to us and have a special meal out together to celebrate the marriage. They agreed and this is what we did. I knew Neal would enjoy this more than having to tolerate the long drive and staying in an unfamiliar hospice.

Loved ones may not appreciate your situation. Sometimes,

we need to steer them to a better understanding, and confiding in a voice of reason can help us make the right choice.

A voice of reason will not just have empathy, but insight and understanding also

We can ask a voice of reason about a dilemma but, to be honest, we usually already know the answer, especially if we feel something is jarring us. Stress often tells us someone may be putting pressure on us or expecting too much. Try not to please too many people, and ask yourself if the situation is in your loved one's or *your* best interest. This will help you to arrive at the right answer.

Over to you...

- Who would be your 'voice of reason'? It might be a close friend or family member, or even a healthcare professional like a community nurse or local doctor.

- If you do have a difficult decision to make and know others will not be happy with your choice, give them reasons for it. We can't please everyone all the time, as much as we would like to. Sometimes we have to accept others may not be happy. Yours and your loved one's best interests also need to be considered.

18

A greater understanding

Over the years, I have been to many carer events and have always enjoyed chatting to others in a similar position. I find carers are selfless and supportive, ready to offer any help and advice when asked. The best thing about speaking to other carers is that they have a better understanding of what you may be going through. They are likely to have experienced many of the situations that you have.

Some years ago, I was very fortunate and privileged to be invited by the Macmillan Charity to No 10 Downing Street – the residence of the Prime Minister for readers outside the UK – for National Carers' Week. All excited, I stood queuing for the event when an older lady just in front of me turned and asked how I was. She then began to share her story. Several years before, her husband had been diagnosed with a neurological condition. At the time, he couldn't handle it and threw himself out of a window to end it all. The fall did not kill him, but it left him severely disabled, as well as having to cope with a degenerative disease.

I found her story appalling and remarked, 'That's awful. I am so sorry. You really have been through it.'

She asked about my caring situation. I then shared my story about Neal's years of ill health. She butted in, 'But he's not the same though, is he?'

Her quick response struck a raw nerve with me. I knew

exactly what she meant. She wasn't talking about his physical health, even though she knew he was bedbound. She was implying that he was perhaps a broken or changed man due to years of suffering. Maybe she had noticed her husband had now inexorably changed.

After being happy one moment at the possibility of meeting the Prime Minister, the next moment I felt tears well up. Anyone else listening would probably not have understood what she meant, but in our brief exchange she clearly displayed a deeper level of understanding that most people did not possess.

Although carers usually have greater insight when it comes to caring, over the years, comments made by friends have made it clear that they had no idea what we were going through. One evening, when Neal was still able to get out and about, we were sat with friends in a bar having a drink. Earlier that week, Neal had had a scan brought forward because he had fallen and had not been quite right since. We were anxious about the results. Meeting our friends took our minds off this, until one of them, a nurse at the local hospital, asked if we'd had the scan results.

'No, not yet,' I replied. 'We should have them next week.'

'As long as you're expecting the worst, that's the main thing,' she said, and nodded her head, agreeing with herself, as if she already knew.

Her hurtful comment felt like a dagger in my chest. It's a good job Neal didn't hear it. A moment before I had been enjoying our get-together. Now I sat, pained with the expectation of a dark fate around the corner and it ruined my night out. This friend, however, carried on chatting to the others unaware of how damaging her remark had been. I sat quietly, feeling detached from the people around me who were drinking and having a good time.

What made her think she knew Neal's scan results, even though she was a nurse? And why would she speak so negatively?

Weren't Neal and I going through enough already? She had clearly assumed the worst. In fact, the following week Neal's scan result was fine. There was nothing drastic we needed to worry about. Did she think it would help me by preparing me for the worst? She needn't have worried on that score – I had learned to be very good at that already!

Perhaps she spoke negatively because she wasn't quite sure what to say. Often people can say the wrong things when they find a topic difficult to talk about. They blurt out a thoughtless comment without realising the harm it can cause. Sadly, the comment can stay with the recipient for years.

Have you noticed any flippant or thoughtless comments made by others whilst you have been caring? I was out with a work colleague one evening, and over a glass of wine told her of the supplements I had just ordered for Neal, to help support his brain.

'What's the point?' she remarked. 'He's going to die anyway.'

That stopped me in my tracks. In the light of her lack of empathy, I decided not to speak about Neal to her again. A few years later, however, I reminded her of what she had said and she looked visibly shocked and apologised. Sometimes we just don't engage our brain before we speak.

If you share your concerns with another, make sure they have empathy for your cause

If you are confiding in another, and disclosing personal information about your loved one's illness and your caring experience, make sure you do so with the right person. When we share our problems with friends, we hope to feel better afterwards, not worse. Furthermore, confiding in the right friends who have understanding and compassion may well elicit helpful solutions.

Over to you...

- Have you socialised with other carers? If you haven't, why not contact your local carers' centre to see what events are coming up? In my experience, carers often have a wealth of knowledge on what is available in your area to help support you. Also, chatting to someone who is going through something similar to yourself can help shed light on issues and may help improve your situation.

- If you catch someone making a flippant comment, instead of quietly allowing it to fester and hurt you, why not speak to this person and let them know how they made you feel?

- When sharing problems and inner thoughts, speak to those with a better understanding, and who do have love and insight into what you are going through.

19

Paid carers – do they actually care?

If a loved one needs help in the home to remain as independent as possible, or you need more help to look after them, you might employ a professional carer or Personal Assistant (PA). Professional carers are either supplied by a care agency or you can employ them directly yourself. Paid carers can be a great help with daily chores, like washing and dressing your loved one, or shopping and preparing meals. If you need a break, a paid carer can look after your loved one whilst you are away.

Over the years, Neal and I had many professional carers come to our home to help with all sorts of tasks, which ranged from hoisting him safely out of bed to taking him to his weekly Egyptology class for the afternoon.

Having employed many paid carers, I can safely say that there are two kinds – those who see it simply as a job, and those who *actually* care. That said, some of the paid carers have been wonderful. They not only cared but we came to regard them as friends. On the other hand, there were a few paid carers who clearly did not care.

One afternoon, a paid carer, Damon, came from a care agency to look after Neal for a few hours. Damon sat with Neal in the garden whilst I was inside the house, working. At this time, Neal often suffered from choking fits due to his neurological condition and, that day, I could hear him having a huge coughing fit in the garden, that just went on and on. Damon was with him, so I assumed that he would help Neal. All our neighbours would have heard Neal's choking. After a short while, I realised the choking hadn't eased and I rushed out to discover what was happening. Although Damon was sat right next to Neal, instead of attending to him, he was busy texting on his mobile phone. He didn't even look up to help. Neal's choking was so loud and so alarming that, if we had been out on the street, I am sure passers-by would have come running to help, but not this carer, who was actually being *paid* to look after Neal. This worried me, because Damon knew I was around, and he knew I could see if he was doing his job, but he still failed. What would have happened if I had not been there at all?

A little while later, Damon had taken Neal back into the living room and I had presumed he was taking care of him and chatting with him. I had continued working in another room. About an hour later, I wandered into the living room to see how things were, only to discover Damon laid out on Neal's hospital bed having a snooze whilst Neal sat slumped in his wheelchair looking glum. Damon soon shot off the bed as I made my feelings known.

I informed the care agency what had happened and we never saw Damon again. I believe he did not have what it took to be a professional carer, because he clearly didn't care about the clients he was supposedly responsible for. We must be able to trust paid carers in our home, especially with our vulnerable loved ones.

There are two kinds of paid carers – those who care and those who don't

Paid care is not cheap and most of us pay for it out of our own pocket, so it is important to ensure you have the right person in your home. The presence of a paid carer is to help lighten the load and alleviate stress. If they are not achieving that, you need to find someone else who can. It can take time to find the right care, but once you have it in place, life will become easier for you and safer for your loved one.

If you take on paid care, make sure the agency or paid carers understand your needs. As always, communication is key. A few clear words can avoid further issues. At times, it may feel like managing staff, but be honest with them and give clear instructions. If a paid carer is causing you problems, tell them, or the care agency. Keeping quiet only exacerbates a situation. They are there to make your life easier.

We need to be able to trust professional carers in our homes

Over the years we used a number of care agencies. The first one started off really well and the paid carers were attentive in helping Neal, but as time went on, there was a high turnover of carers. Many didn't stay long and it appeared they were not happy with the agency. As soon as I had trained one carer up, so they knew what needed to be done for Neal, they were gone. The agency carers were not cheap and it didn't seem to matter that I spent time and energy greeting new carers and talking through everything that needed to be done, only never to see them again.

Unfortunately, this wasn't the only issue, and problems began to escalate, not only with the carers, but with the agency itself. They took up more of my time and it became very stressful. So, as mentioned in the chapter, 'Straight talking', when a service started to let me down, I then kept a log of the issues that arose, including date, time, who had been involved and what had gone wrong. Why was I logging this build-up of issues? Weeks later,

I just wouldn't remember everything that had happened. The final straw came when one of the agency carers refused to shave Neal or help with the bedding. As he just stood there, I found myself doing everything that morning and asked him what was the point of him being there.

I complained to the agency and to the local authority, whose job it was to hire them onto their roster. I refused to use care agencies again and turned instead to employing private carers. I am so pleased that I did. Not only were they cheaper, as there were no management or office staff taking their cut, but they really did care and, as I mentioned, I have remained friends with them to this day.

The really lovely thing about hiring private carers was that there was no high turnover. Some of them came to care for Neal for years. After his stroke, when Neal was unable to speak, these carers knew Neal's personality and humour from before, and they continued chatting to him, as they had done previously, even though he couldn't reply. It would have been comforting for Neal to continue to have these familiar and friendly faces caring for him, and they knew what he liked and didn't like, even if he couldn't communicate verbally anymore.

Paid care is there to help, not to hinder

Although cheaper, there are downsides to hiring paid carers individually – you have to organise them and ensure you have back up, in case they are unable to turn up. You also need insurance to keep you and them covered whilst they are under your roof.

Even though I had trouble with care agencies, others have found them absolutely fine. If you do, that's wonderful. The important thing is to voice any concerns and not put up with poor care. The right care in your home will not only alleviate stress but help to give you a break.

Over to you...

- If you are wondering whether to have paid carers in your home, speak to charities who support carers, or others caring for loved ones in your local area, to find out whom they use. Are there any particular care agencies or private carers they recommend?

- Can you obtain any funding for professional care? We paid for carers for years until Neal became very ill, after which we received funding, which was called Continuing Healthcare.

- If you use paid carers, are you happy with them? Are they meeting your needs? If not, have a word with them or with the care agency that employs them. Giving negative feedback can feel awkward when you have a carer in your home, but remember, they are there to help.

- If you have had to put your loved one into a care home and you are unhappy with the level of care, let them know. Don't put up with poor care.

SECTION 4

Your health and wellbeing

20

Getting your 40 winks?

We all need sleep. It is a vital part of our daily life and keeps us both physically and mentally well. Sleep is vital for our health, memory, mood and energy. Having enough sleep (see below) keeps us more alert during the day and able to make better decisions.

Having enough sleep can be a tricky business for carers. Restless nights can be filled with worry about a loved one and other knock-on problems. I have ended up exhausted by doing too much in the day and then worrying all night. The following morning, tired and anxious, I could sometimes feel my heart racing. Struggling to cope, because my mind wasn't as sharp, I made wrong decisions or even hurt myself whilst not focusing properly on moving and handling Neal.

As mentioned in my story, every night I used a baby monitor to listen out for Neal. I slept with one ear open for years, just in case. Some nights, I would race downstairs to attend to Neal because he was having a coughing fit. Broken sleep left me feeling drained for days afterwards and affected my mood.

There can be various reasons why carers end up having sleepless nights. For example, if your loved one suffers from dementia, they may go walkabout in the middle of the night. If you experience this, there are devices and systems that can be set up in your home to alert you when they are out of bed. This can help you to sleep better, knowing you will be woken if you are needed.

Most of us need around eight hours of good quality sleep a night to function properly; some may need a little more or a little less.

Sleep is vital in keeping us healthy, both physically and mentally

Sleep boosts your immunity

Did you know that lack of sleep affects the immune system? It can leave you vulnerable to any bugs or colds going around – the last thing you need when caring for someone who is unwell. Sleep loss not only plays a part in whether we become susceptible to viruses, but also affects how we fight illness.

If you are struggling to get the right amount of sleep, there are a number of things you can do to improve the quality of your sleep:

- Make sure your bedroom is comfortable – not too hot, cold or noisy. Try having the window open at night to breathe in fresh air.
- Try not to have your computer or TV in your bedroom.
- Ensure your bedroom is dark enough, as light can prevent your brain making enough of the natural hormone, melatonin. This is a natural antioxidant and tells your body when to sleep.
- Take regular exercise. Swimming or walking are more relaxing exercises, but try not to exercise too near to bedtime, as this may raise your core temperature just when it should be reducing slightly, and keep you awake.

- Examine your mattress. It should be firm enough to support you comfortably, but not so firm that you feel perched on top of it.
- Cut down on tea and coffee from 16:00 onwards because these contain caffeine which increases adrenaline levels in the body and lowers the chemicals that encourage sleep.
- Don't eat or drink a lot late at night. Have your evening meal relatively early, if you can.
- Spend time relaxing before you go to bed – a warm bath can help. There are many relaxation techniques. Try listening to guided meditation audios or reading books. Relaxation classes, like yoga or meditation, can help.
- If you can, try keeping a regular pattern of going to bed and rising at the same time every day, even if you are not always tired at the appointed hour.
- Keep a notepad by your bed so that, if you are worried about something in the middle of the night, you can write it down then and there, instead of trying to remember it, helping to clear your mind.
- If you still cannot sleep, don't lie there worrying. There are many great guided meditations or ambient music CDs available which can help to send you off.
- Breathing techniques at bedtime can also help. Most of us just breathe shallowly, but taking steady slow breaths and continuing to focus on them can help quieten the mind:
  1. Whilst lying in bed, close your mouth and breathe through your nose for a count of four.
  2. Hold your breath for a count of four.
  3. Then exhale completely through your mouth for a count of eight and repeat.

If you feel like a snooze in the middle of the day and are able to have one, then do so. However, don't sleep for too long in case it messes up your body clock. Listening to your body is a good way of knowing when to rest so you can keep yourself well.

Positive down-time

When I had had a particularly exhausting day and was feeling low, as I climbed into bed, I would think of 10 things I was grateful for that day. It might just have been a hot shower, Neal's love or things I was looking forward to. This not only helped remind me of the good things in life, but shifted my mood to a better place before sleeping.

You may be wondering what you have to be thankful for at present. Energy grows where your thoughts flow – so worrying and stressing about a situation can make it feel worse than it may actually be. Thinking about all the things you actually do have can shift your focus and make you feel better before having a good night's sleep. Thinking of great friends and family, a nice comfy bed, or the sun shining that day, can make us realise there is still a lot we have to be thankful for.

> *'Sleep is the best meditation'*
>
> Dalai Lama

Over to you...

- How many hours of sleep do you need each night to feel fully rested the next morning?
- There are a number of ideas listed in this chapter on how to improve the quality of your sleep (see pages 168-169) to keep you healthier and your mood lighter. Try a few out to see which work best for you.

21

Sex and intimacy

Human touch can boost another's wellbeing, especially when caring. Putting your arm around another, holding their hand or giving them a hug can speak volumes. It gives us connection, love and support. In today's society, the importance of human touch is often overlooked. Many of us connect through social media or email, but face-to-face contact and physical touch benefit everyone, especially carers, who often feel isolated whilst caring for another.

The power of a hug

How do you feel after a hug? Hugging another person can make us feel supported and relaxed. It can also give us an emotional lift. Did you know that hugging is not only good for us emotionally, but physically too? Research has shown that hugging can help heal by strengthening the immune system. It also decreases stress and tension in the body, whilst releasing feel-good hormones like oxytocin into the brain.

Once Neal was up, and in his wheelchair, I would hug him for several minutes and I could feel him completely relax into my arms. It felt like a relief for him as we connected both physically and emotionally. Hugging was our way of communicating and bonding, especially once he couldn't speak. Human touch can reach someone even if they are in a dark and difficult place.

Having a proper hug, where hearts are pressed together, can build trust and a sense of security. It has also been shown to raise serotonin levels. Years ago, when I came home from a difficult day at work in a bad mood, Neal would often call out to me, 'Come and hug the hate away!'

I couldn't but smile and put my arms around him. This instantly made me feel better.

Sex – sadly a taboo subject for many carers

If you care for a spouse or partner who has physically or mentally changed, sex can seem a distant memory and your relationship may have considerably altered. Also, if they are incontinent, this can add further difficulties to intimacy.

Neal took many drugs for his illness and some dampened his libido. As he became physically disabled, sex became a thing of the past. This was sad for both of us, as we lost a part of our lives that we had previously enjoyed together. Neal's health, or rather illness, became our main priority. After years of chemotherapy and steroids, he also gained weight and he didn't feel well much of the time, so I didn't blame him for not wanting to have sex. His reply was always a resounding 'No', which deeply saddened me. Neal's personality had changed and his body and health had deteriorated. Sadly, sex became the elephant in the room.

I had had no idea how much caring would impact my own life. I endured a sexless marriage throughout most of my 30s and into my early 40s, and I missed it from day one. It meant a lack of intimacy – an important aspect of a relationship. I continued to love Neal very much, but our relationship had inevitably changed.

I know it can be difficult for the cared-for, when it comes to intimacy, but it is also difficult for the carer, and this is often overlooked. It can be hard enough to be a carer, but to miss out on an important aspect of a relationship can be a further hardship. I once heard a husband caring for his wife say, 'You have all the responsibilities of a marriage but none of the perks.'

Many carers will feel frustrated, resentful, or even angry at this change in their relationship. Although carers try to do their best, they may feel penalised for doing the right thing, by being there for their loved one, in the knowledge that they are missing out on something which should be normal, healthy and enjoyable.

Years ago, at a carers' outing organised by a local charity, I met a fellow carer of a similar age who had been caring for his wife for years. His wife was disabled due to a neurological condition. He asked me if I fancied meeting for a coffee the following week. I looked forward to chewing the cud about life with someone in a similar position, especially as he was my own age.

We met on a lovely sunny day, alfresco at a coffee shop. As we started to chat, hardly five minutes had passed before he sat back in his chair, closed his eyes and told me there was something he wanted to talk about. I sensed instantly where he was headed and leaned forward, looking straight at his closed eyes. I spoke in a low key, 'Oh, I know what you're going to talk about.'

My hunch was right. He had met me because his marriage had been dogged by his wife's illness and it had been sexless for years. He had wanted to meet up to see if I was interested in an intimate relationship with him, especially as he knew my spouse was equally disabled. I just hadn't expected this to be on the cards that day, otherwise I would not have met him. I made it clear I was not keen on his suggestion and we both sat back with an air of disappointment at how our lives had turned out. I look back at that day and think how brave it was of him to ask, but I did also feel for his wife.

I have often wondered what other carers do about this difficult subject. I have heard a number of stories of how carers have dealt with sex whilst looking after a spouse. One was of a wife, who cared for her husband. He was disabled and using a wheelchair. Whilst the wife continued to care for him, she had taken a lover. Not only did the husband know of their relationship, but he was apparently fine with it. At the time of hearing this, I remember thinking, 'Blimey! That's a tall order for the husband.'

Then I started to think about his wife. She had been caring for her husband for years, and continued to do so. By having an intimate relationship with another man, she may have found what had been lacking in their marriage for all those years. Could this extra-marital relationship have given her the happiness and support she needed, as well as the strength to continue a difficult life of caring for years to come? It was a decision only she could make and it was certainly not for me to judge.

I am aware many would not agree with this arrangement. Most of us who are caring for a husband or wife would feel a sense of duty to be faithful, and would not want to feel we are betraying our loved one. Personally, I cannot judge others, unless I have walked in their shoes and know exactly how they have been feeling. We all have different needs and when these are met, we have more to give to others. It is a personal decision.

Many will relate to this difficult topic. I am aware it's not quite the same, but having a hug or just holding hands on a regular basis can relieve stress and anxiety whilst making your connection stronger. I hugged and kissed Neal several times every day, whether he liked it or not! Whenever I did, we both felt instantly better.

Over to you...

- How do you feel when you are hugged? Is this something you can do more of with your loved ones?

- Each carer is different and the relationship with the cared-for is also unique. Are your needs being met on an emotional and physical level? If not, could you openly discuss your feelings with your loved one? We often have to be brave to start a conversation and it is not always easy, but being honest and connecting with your loved one can help bridge gaps.

22

Take a break

We all need regular breaks, whether from caring, from work, or from our usual daily routine. Taking ourselves away, for quality time out, can make us feel more alive and help to recharge our batteries. Having a break is good for our wellbeing.

Depending on how your loved one is, holidays may be a distant memory. Also, all too often the cared-for's needs come first and everything else comes second. You may feel you can't leave your loved one or you don't have time to have a break. They need you, right?

Imagine you have received an urgent call and you are needed 60 miles away. You climb into your car and notice the petrol gauge is hovering just above empty, but you ignore this. You don't have time to fill up, because you need to be somewhere important as soon as possible. You are already late in setting off and don't want to let others down. They may be angry with you if you're late.

You turn on the ignition and set off. A little while later, you are pulling onto the motorway with an almost empty tank. How long does it take before you hear the engine cough and splutter and then die? You have run out of petrol, and you're in the middle lane of the motorway, so you drift over onto the hard shoulder while traffic whizzes by you at top speed. Left stranded, not only are you unable to arrive at your destination, but you have put yourself at risk.

On top of that, you have to call for help. You call the breakdown emergency number and draw in others to come and assist you. Not only have you not arrived at your destination, but now others have had to come to your rescue.

Whilst caring, many carers' fuel gauges hover just above empty. We ignore our health, even when we are not feeling well, because there is something more pressing – our loved one. It can be very difficult to take a break whilst caring. We want the best for those we look after, and so we ignore our own needs, leaving ourselves drained. If this is you, how long will it be before *you* finally break down and others have to come to your rescue?

Arranging respite care

It can be difficult to take a break, especially if you struggle to find cover. We can ask family or friends to come and help, but this is not always easy. They are often busy with their own lives and may live some distance away.

If you cannot persuade family to come and help whilst you have a break, you could organise a paid carer to look after your loved one. This, of course, will depend on your finances. Otherwise, hospices offer respite care, and can give a longer break. Charities also offer befriending services, so you may be able to go out for at least a few hours each week whilst someone sits with your loved one.

There are also day centres in the community, where loved ones can be looked after once a week, giving you time off from caring. Some charities even offer holiday apartments for both the carer and the cared-for to have time away together. Search online or ask local charities if they offer respite care, or if they know of anyone else who does.

Don't feel guilty!

Many carers turn down the offer of having a break because they feel guilty leaving their loved one. How can you enjoy yourself whilst the cared-for remains ill at home? Many carers feel that they don't need valuable time out – but if this is you, you still need a break now and then. It will not only do *you* good, but also your loved one. A break will make you feel rested and in a good frame of mind and able to give your loved one better care and attention.

Also, carers often refuse a break because they believe care provided by someone else will not be as good. You maintain a high level of caring and you know exactly what your loved one needs and how they need it. Hospitals, hospices, nursing homes and even other family members are unlikely to have the same expertise as you in providing care for your loved one. However, you *still* need a break. If you refuse to take time out and deplete yourself further, you may end up ill and be forced to take a break. So do try to have time to yourself.

I noticed that, if I didn't take time out, even for a few hours a week, I would end up feeling quite flat. I felt more like a robot – purely existing for another. Having a break took not only my body, but also my mind, away from living with a terminally ill husband. We need our space. Also, if we become over-absorbed in our role, our individuality can start to disappear.

Christmas or big holidays can be particularly draining, and many carers fall ill immediately afterwards. For years, every January I fell ill. One year, I recall desperately trying to book Neal in for respite care straight after Christmas. I was already worn out and poorly. I was dismayed to discover that there was a waiting list of nearly three months. At that time, I was already on my knees. I should have booked him in sooner. That was a hard lesson learned.

The nurse at the hospice told me that waiting until you are sick before having a break defeated the object of respite care. Carers need to have regular breaks to keep themselves healthy. After enduring months of illness, I made sure I kept to this.

Get them on your side

Although you may desperately need a break to get away, your loved one may not be as understanding. They may have become so used to your being there for them, that having someone else step in whilst you are gone will be uncomfortable for them. It may leave them feeling vulnerable. When Neal went to the day centre at our local hospice once a week, as well as giving me a break, he would be checked over to see if he had any health issues. The hospice also offered longer respite care and I used to book Neal in for a week, so that I could have a proper holiday now and then. Neal was never keen on going in, but I made it clear I needed this time and that I would soon be home again. He was quite good at agreeing most of the time.

One particular respite week, I was lucky enough to go skiing with friends in the Alps. I remember standing in the fresh snow with the sun on my face, smiling and relaxing. All I had to do that week was think about myself and make the most of it. I felt alive! The next day I gave Neal a call at the hospice to see how he was and tell him I was thinking of him. I was in for a shock. 'Get back here now!' he yelled down the phone.

My eyes widened. Neal *never* yelled. 'I can't, Neal. I'm in the Alps,' I whimpered.

He then hung up on me.

I was distraught. Tears flowed and I went about my day feeling low. I knew Neal didn't want to spend a week in the hospice, but I had explained thoroughly why I needed a break. I made it clear that I would be there for him when I returned. As this call had upset me and I was aware Neal was lying there angry with me, I wondered what I could do. In that moment, I wouldn't enjoy any of my time away, so I called his family and asked them if they could call Neal once a day to check everything was alright. They agreed, which took the weight off my mind.

When I returned from holiday, I was concerned how Neal would receive me when I collected him, but he was fine. I think he was just relieved I was back.

If you come up against resistance from your loved one, try explaining that you need to remain healthy so that you can continue being there for them. Without a break, you could become drained and ill, which is not good for either of you. You want to give your loved one your best.

If the cared-for is not used to you spending time away from them, try having short breaks of a few hours, reassuring them that you will not be long. If you familiarise them with your not being at home all of the time, you can then try extending your absence for longer.

Going into the outside space can give you time to reflect on the inside space

What would happen if you never had a break? I know of an elderly man who cares for his wife. He cares for her at all times, *never* having a break. On the odd occasion when he needs to leave the house to go for an urgent health appointment, he leaves his wife with someone she knows. Because she is dependent on her husband, she has wailed for hours in his absence. Friends and paid carers have tried to calm her down, but she is beside herself if her husband is not with her. This co-dependency is not good for anyone, including his wife, given the stress she endures.

Is socialising an effort?

If you haven't been out to see friends in a while, it can seem like hard work. You may need to organise everything for your loved one before you head out and, even then, you may not feel particularly sociable. Sometimes I had to push myself to go out, but I was always glad that I had. Seeing your friends can help you maintain a healthy social and support network, allowing you to get through the challenging times, now and in the future. You never know when your caring role may come to an end and, if and when it does, you will need your friends.

When you are in the thick of caring, you just can't see the wood for the trees. Taking time away, even for a short while, can help us gain clarity on our caring situation. Often we do not realise how much it is affecting us. Stepping back, we are then able to make better decisions for everyone concerned.

Don't forget other loved ones

Putting all my love and attention into one person cost me dearly. I was so absorbed in caring for Neal that not only did I fall ill but, whilst I was recovering, I learnt of my grandfather's death. I was gutted. I realised I hadn't been home to see my family for over a year. They only lived a two-hour drive away. Not only had I allowed my caring duties to take over my life and health, but I had forgotten how much the rest of my family meant to me. There were certain loved ones I hadn't seen in over a year and now one of them was gone forever.

I vowed never to put all my love into just one person again. I knew Neal was my husband and needed my love and support, but I still deserved to have a relationship with the rest of my family and they needed my love too. All our loved ones are important, not just the cared-for.

Take a breather

For many carers, the only break they allow themselves each day, is when they fall into bed exhausted every night. But if you do take even short breaks, such as 10 minutes between chores, and pace yourself throughout the day, you are more likely to feel better and more rested.

Where can you factor in a breather each day and what could you do with those precious minutes? Sitting in the garden, having a lie down or chatting to a friend on the phone, can all help break up the monotony.

Whenever I was out of the house, even for a short while, it would make me feel better. I remember once smiling to myself on a train station platform, relieved to be outside and on my own for a bit. This is no reflection on Neal. I loved him dearly, but I still needed the fresh air and time to myself.

A carer for her husband once told me that going into outside space gave her time to reflect on her inside space.

Look on having time out as an MOT. When we are caught up in life, we do not realise how much it is affecting us. Stepping back with regular breaks helps us to take stock and even to enjoy ourselves. Give yourself permission and have a break. You will then feel more rested and better equipped to care for your loved one.

Over to you...

- When you get into bed at night, how do you feel? Do you feel exhausted? If you do, try resting between chores each day to have 'me time'.

- When was the last time you took a longer break? If you haven't had one in a while, why not ask your local carers' centre or doctor how you can access support, so you can take time away? Are there family members who could come and take the reins, even for a day, to give you time away from home?

- Do you have regular breaks to see friends and so your cared-for can become used to your absence? Can you make this a weekly occurrence?

- If you struggle to find cover for a break, why not invite friends or family over to do something enjoyable with them?

- You could have a list ready of the things you enjoy doing, so, if you have only 15 minutes free, for example, you can make the most of it.

23

How much longer?

I asked myself this question many times whilst caring. I also know of other carers who have asked themselves this same question: 'How much longer am I going to be caring for my loved one? And how much longer *can* I keep caring?'

If you have asked yourself this question, this is not a bad reflection on you or your loved one. Even if your cared-for is patient and understanding whilst you attend to them, these days, months and years will not be back and you want to make the most of your life. You may even feel guilty asking this question. You know that if your caring role comes to an end, this will probably mean that your loved one has passed, or has become resident in a care home. Such thoughts can be conflicting and unsettling.

We want to make the most of our time with our loved ones, but we want to make the most of our own lives too, as I have said. Even with conflicting priorities, we need to keep a sense of perspective and strike a balance between living our own life whilst caring for theirs.

If someone had told me Neal would survive 13 years with a malignant brain tumour, I would have been surprised. Historical statistics suggested that he would be lucky to live for 18 months. Because the prognosis was so poor, and I knew he could be gone any moment, I gave him my all. His years of ill health rolled by, together with the years of my own life.

As much as I loved my husband, my life was happening there and then and, as he deteriorated, I became absorbed by his illness, neglecting my own needs. He was my world and my perspective on life narrowed. As his world became smaller, so did mine. I felt myself emotionally holding him tighter, and I slowly sank with him. I remember crying on his shoulder as he sat slumped in his wheelchair. It was unhealthy for both of us and I can't imagine what he must have been thinking. My health suffered as a consequence. It was then that I realised I needed to allow space between caring for Neal and caring for my own needs. Although we were very close, we were still two separate beings. As hard as it is to imagine losing a loved one, we are all born and we all die at different times. Neal's time would probably come sooner than mine and I had to accept this. I needed to create space for my own life, so that I could be there for both of us.

Don't let your present circumstances rob you of your future

Right now, how much longer do you think you can care for your loved one? A year? Three years? Five years? *More?* These numbers may sound daunting, but asking yourself this question can alert you to how well you are coping at present. If you feel like throwing your hands up in the air and saying, 'Not for another week!' then this is a good indication that you need to ask for more support now, or make changes in your daily life to give yourself a breathing space.

If you have been caring for years, you may wonder whether there will be any time left for you at the end of it all. We can't predict the future so making the right choices *now*, for *both* of you, will help keep you well and make the most of the days.

Many carers feel their lives are on hold and that once their loved one has gone, they can embark upon what they really want to do in life. What if this happens to be years ahead? If there are things you want to do and places you want to go now, why not ask family, friends, local charities or social services to help you find a solution? It's not always easy, but looking for alternative caring arrangements for your loved one can help you achieve at least some of your goals.

Time waits for no man

When I was sat in a wellbeing group at my local charity, I asked about our friend, Penny, whom I had not seen at the group for several months. Penny was an elderly lady with a neurological condition similar to Parkinson's, and she had dyskinesia – severe uncontrollable shakes. That day, a woman sitting nearby told me she had recently attended Penny's funeral. I was saddened at the news, but the next piece of news was even more alarming.

I immediately thought of her husband who had appeared fit and well whenever he had slowly walked Penny into the centre. I had never had a chance to speak to him, as he had always left immediately after dropping her off – clearly for some time out. When I asked how he was coping with Penny's death, the reply was almost flippant: 'Oh, he died about six months ago.'

You owe it to yourself to find time every day to enjoy yourself. It's your life too

I was shocked. The cared-for had outlived the carer. Everybody that day was saddened by the news of Penny's death, but no one seemed particularly bothered about the husband, who had cared for her all those years. She was a lovely lady, but caring for someone with continuous severe shakes looked exhausting. Had the pressure of caring for someone so ill for so long taken its ultimate toll?

Caring can quickly take over your life and before you know it, another year has passed without seeing good friends and family. Instead of allowing this time to drift and relationships with others to become distant, it's worth making the effort to keep in touch with them. We don't then feel so isolated.

Over to you...

- Do you feel your caring responsibilities have taken precedence over your relationships with friends and family? Do you meet up with them? If it proves difficult, could you try calling or Skyping them instead on a more regular basis?

- Is there anything you would really like to do, but have been putting off due to caring? Asking for support could not only lighten your load, but also give you time to achieve some of your goals and to do things you enjoy.

SECTION 5

Enjoying your life

24

Focus on the good stuff

When you see a bee buzzing about the garden or in a park, what do you notice about it? The bee will head straight to one beautiful flower and then to another. Once it has visited one flower and collected the pollen, it heads straight for another to do the same. If there is rubbish nearby, or dirt and squalor, do you see the bee heading straight for it to take a look? No, it will keep buzzing from one flower to the next. Once it has exhausted the flora in that area, it heads off to look for more.

In comparison, if you were to see exposed rubbish, rotten food or even faecal matter lying strewn around, you can guess there would be a handful of flies sitting around on top of it. If there were beautiful flowers nearby, would they dart straight over to take a look? No, this is not what they focus on. Their focus is rotten and decaying matter.

In comparison, if you were to visit a park full of beautiful flowers, though it also had a bit of rubbish strewn in a few places, which would *you* focus on? The good stuff, or the bad?

Whilst caring, it is easy to focus on the bad stuff. A loved one may be ill and there will be a lot to contend with. Not long after Neal was diagnosed, we headed out one evening to meet good friends at a local restaurant. Neal was on chemotherapy and we hadn't seen our friends in a while. Because they cared, they took an interest in his condition and the treatment he was receiving.

I had attended all Neal's oncology appointments with him, so I indulged them with all the details of the chemotherapy, because I am an expert now, right?

I explained to them all about brain tumours in great detail and about the radiotherapy and chemotherapy. After a while, Neal butted in, 'Can we talk about something else? I've come out to have a good time.'

Abstaining from enjoyment will not bring out the best in you

I stopped speaking. He was right. We had come out to enjoy the evening and escape from the illness, hospitals and prognosis. We were meant to enjoy a relaxing night out and focus on the good stuff. I apologised to Neal and we moved on to more uplifting topics for the rest of the evening.

If friends ask what is happening with your loved one's health, it's good to let them know, but if your number one topic of conversation is the illness and all that is associated with it, no one will benefit. Consistently focusing on a difficult or negative situation will depress not only you, but also friends and family. It could even alienate you from them. For example, if you were to hear a friend consistently discuss a marriage break up or family feud, every time you met them, it would take the joy out of the evening. You would probably find it draining. It's good to catch up and talk about these things, but not if you become completely *absorbed* by them.

After that particular evening, when friends or family asked about Neal's health, I would give them a quick update, but then move on to other things. We wanted to enjoy our time together – to be in the moment, and focus on the good things in life that we still had together.

Being in the moment

Most of us are either dwelling in the past or worrying about the future, but all we really have is the here and now – this very moment. Whether you are making dinner, laughing with a friend, or caring for a loved one, in these moments we can be fully present and make the most of this time. None of us knows what the future holds and it doesn't help to fret about the past, as this has gone. Being in the moment can help us enjoy our days with our cared-for and help us feel more at ease. Enjoying the now will help to shift our mood and alleviate stress.

How often do you live in the present moment? Are you too busy thinking of what might happen, or about the past? Most of us rarely give ourselves time to enjoy the moment. Just doing something as simple as having a cup of tea, and enjoying the moment for what it is, can bring us back to ourselves and help us unwind.

'If you are depressed, you are living in the past.
If you are anxious, you are living in the future.
If you are at peace, you are living in the present.'

Lao Tzu

Have you noticed that time really does fly when you are having fun? Watching a good film or laughing with friends can seem to whiz by in seconds. This is because we have been living in the moment. It is a great place to be. Often, when we walk in nature, and focus on our surroundings, this can help bring us into the here and now. Everything else can then seem distant.

Have you noticed how young children play? They run around together, laughing and smiling. They live for the moment.

What brings you into *your* present moment? When do you find time flies? What good stuff do you enjoy focusing on? It's good to take your mind away from the difficulties in life.

Be focus aware

When Neal was first diagnosed, he was at home all day whilst I was out at work. He watched a lot of television. As well as enjoying nature programmes, he began to watch the news channels, over and over again. He stared at the telly as BBC News 24 Live, with its grim stories, continuously replayed on a loop.

News channels often sensationalise negative stories and repeat them over and over again, especially if something truly awful has happened. Like a car crash, you can't help but look. Neal was hooked for hours every day, and it wasn't doing him any good, especially as he was very ill. At that time, the main news story was a big recession that was hitting the UK. The TV screen displayed a huge red arrow directed downwards, as it recounted the depressing details of job losses and cuts.

One evening, as I came home from work and walked into the living room, Neal looked up from the sofa, very worried. 'The recession is still hitting hard,' he informed me. 'People are losing their jobs and homes.'

I gazed down at him, concerned. Not so much about the recession, but rather about him. He was dealing with brain cancer and I felt he didn't need to fret about the recession as well. 'But you don't have a job to lose, Neal, and you have your home. You are safe,' I replied. I picked up the remote control and flicked over the channels.

'Which comedy would you like to watch?' I asked him and clicked onto *Seinfeld*, a comedy he loved. I then sat down to enjoy it with him. It's good to know what is happening around the world, but not to the point of becoming obsessed with depressing news, giving us more to worry about.

How do you feel after watching particular TV programmes? Which make you feel happy, and which make you feel sad or anxious? Some programmes uplift us, whilst others can leave us feeling low. Being aware of our mood after watching certain programmes can help us to make better choices, ensuring we are left feeling more positive, rather than drained.

An attitude of gratitude

It's easy to dwell on the difficulties, but focusing on what you still have can help you to enjoy every day. Furthermore, having gratitude can help you feel better. When I have struggled, I have made myself list things I am thankful for that day, and I have always felt better for it. If you try this, once you get going, the list can become endless. Even though Neal has gone, I am still thankful that he was in my life and that I did my best for him. I'm even grateful that you are reading this right now, and if it helps to improve your life in any way, I am even more grateful.

Nip it in the bud

Apparently, whenever we start a train of thought, within 17 seconds it can have us gripped. Time can then fly as this thought takes us on a full-on ride, and before we realise it, half an hour may have passed. When you start to worry about something, how long does your train of thought run? Five minutes? An hour? All day?

Falling into a groove of worrying or being angry about a situation can set off neurogenesis (the creation of new connections) in the brain. The more you think of that one thing, the more connections are created. This negative circuitry then strengthens and pulls you in more easily.

Say, for example, someone consistently thinks of something that makes them angry. Every time they think this thought, the neurons in the brain fire and wire. The more they dwell on this angry thought, the more their brain compensates and connects even more neurons to help them. This individual may become so stuck in this thought process that it becomes a habit. Pushing this further, if they are unaware of the habit and it continues, it can become a feature of their personality.

It's good to air our issues but not to become obsessed by them

Now and then, we all find ourselves stuck in a groove of negative thoughts. If you notice one in particular and want to nip it in the bud, try putting an elastic band around your wrist. Every time you think of that thought, ping it. This can pull you out of an habitual negative thought pattern. I have tried this many times, especially when I want to stop thinking about something that does not serve me, and it has worked for me.

Changing the way you look at things

When Neal's oncologist decided to take him off chemotherapy, because it was leaving him fatigued, I knew it was probably for the best, but it still scared the hell out of me. Neal and I believed the treatment had kept his brain tumour at bay and him alive. What if stopping the chemo would see the tumour return? Nobody can remain on chemotherapy forever, so there was only one way to find out. Neal came off the treatment, which we both found unsettling.

A few weeks later we decided to go to a brain tumour support group. The group was made up of patients with brain tumours and their families. As I sat down, I started to chat to a lovely Japanese lady, who looked to be in her late 40s. As I shared my worries about Neal discontinuing his treatment, the lady shared a valuable insight that helped me see the situation very differently. She had previously been diagnosed with a brain tumour. I was surprised to hear this as she looked so well.

I would not have guessed. She had also stopped chemotherapy, not knowing what the future would bring. Although she had previously worried that she might fall ill again, she eventually got over this by focusing on living.

'We can either keep worrying about the disease, or focus on the here and now and make the most of our lives,' she said. 'Now I just get on with living.'

Don't think about what you can't do; think about what you can do

Her insight made me feel better. She continued to tell me that we can waste time and energy speculating on what might happen, and even expecting the worst, but it will not do us any good. She now lived each day at a time, so much so that she had decided not to go for further MRI brain scans. Not everyone would feel comfortable with this, but it was her personal journey. I loved her attitude to life. She was aspiring to enjoy her time, and she looked good on it. She focused on living.

As hard as caring and life can be at times, the best we can do is make the most of life, and focus on the good stuff. There is always something to be grateful for, every day.

Over to you...

- Do you notice yourself talking about, or even being obsessed, with your loved one's condition or other problems on a daily basis? If so, can you catch yourself as you start to worry, and shift your thoughts onto something more positive or enjoyable? Becoming aware of your regular thought patterns can be the first step to turning your attention to better things.

- To boost your mood, you could try creating a relaxing environment around you by:
  - o Listening to calming music
  - o Taking up a hobby
  - o Using positive self-talk. Many of our daily thoughts are negative as we live in survival mode – pre-empting any issues that could arise to attempt to keep ourselves safe. Instead, speak kindly and supportively to yourself, recognising how well you are doing.
- There are also many inspirational and positive talks on YouTube. I love listening to Anita Moorjani or Dr Wayne Dyer. They always talk a lot of sense, leaving me feeling uplifted.
- If you can, play games with your loved one – cards, board-games, Jenga. What fun things could you do together?
- Having gratitude can quickly help lift our mood. What and who are you grateful for in your life? Noticing what you do have will shift your mood to a better place.
- If you notice a particular negative thought that keeps popping up, try putting an elastic band around one wrist and twanging it every time this thought arises. See if this helps to steer you away from any looping and draining thoughts.
- Celebrate the small victories. Remind yourself that all your efforts matter. You are not responsible for how everything turns out. You can only do your best. Your love is the best thing you can give to another.

25

A true story of transformation

Focusing on your own health and wellbeing may sound like a huge overhaul, but it really isn't. The following true story demonstrates that just the smallest of changes can create the biggest of differences, making life much easier to bear.

Christine's story

Christine wakes early, climbs out of her single bed and heads downstairs. She is in her mid 30s, petite, pretty, with shoulder-length blonde hair and this weekend she is back at her parents' house in Holland.

As she stands looking out of the kitchen window, waiting for the kettle to boil, she feels a knot in her stomach and senses a heaviness in the air. She views the garden and notices it has not been tended to for some time and is now overgrown. Hardly surprising. On the floor to her right is a pile of dirty laundry – something else to take care of.

She hears the click of the kitchen door open behind her, and as she turns, she sees her father pushing her mother in a wheelchair, into the kitchen. Her father is in his mid 70s, tall and wiry with short white hair and a short white beard. He has dark bags under his eyes and the corners of his lips are turned downwards. He is already dressed, wearing a grey shirt and navy trousers. As he wheels his wife to the kitchen table, Christine can see the caring has taken its toll on him. He has been caring for her mother for over 20 years, ever since she was diagnosed with multiple sclerosis.

Her mother, in her late 60s, has short brown hair, and sits quietly in her wheelchair and half smiles at Christine.

'Right, let's get your medication and breakfast,' her father states irritably.

Christine stands to watch in silence as her father prepares her mother's breakfast. Once it is ready, he brings a bowl of porridge to the table, sits down and starts to spoon-feed her mother in silence.

Christine notices how roughly her father feeds her mother. It is very matter-of-fact, another job to be done. He feeds her out of obligation, nothing more.

Once he has finished, he grabs his shoes from the corner of the kitchen, laces them up and finds his jacket hanging in the hallway. Without a word, he opens the kitchen door and leaves the house. Christine peers out of the window to see him cycling down the garden on his pushbike and off down the road.

She turns and comes to sit with her mother, holding her hand. They smile at one another, but she sees a pained expression on her mother's face. Life is not good and it hasn't been for a long time.

Christine sits and chats with her mother, telling her of all her news from back in London, where she now lives and works. After a while, her mother's neck becomes tired, a side effect of her condition. It starts to droop and eventually hangs down onto her chest. It looks uncomfortable. Not only that, Christine now finds herself talking to the top of her mother's head. As she asks her mother if she should put the headrest onto the chair to bring her head up and support her neck, her mother replies, 'Oh, don't worry about me. I'm okay'.

But Christine can see that things are not okay.

Around lunchtime, her father reappears after his bike ride. Whilst her mother rests in another room, Christine decides to have a chat with her father, as she is worried for both of them. 'How are things, Papa?' she enquires.

Her father lets out a huge sigh as he sits looking at his hands in his lap with a furrowed brow. 'You know I love your mother very much, but I feel so drained. I am at the end of my tether. I feel I am purely existing for your mother, and when she is gone, I will be gone.'

These words upset Christine. She is heading home tomorrow, leaving her father caring for her declining mother. She worries things are likely to get worse.

Later that week, Christine is at a networking evening in London where a few speakers get up to tell their stories to help others. The topic of the night is 'Making the world a better place'. Christine watches as I tell my story from the stage of caring for Neal and how I made *his* world a better place. As I finish and step down, Christine comes running towards me.

'I loved your talk, Sara. I would really like your advice. Could we meet up later this week?' I smile at Christine and we exchange contact details to meet.

The following Wednesday morning, I walk into the small café in Richmond. I can smell the coffee and the murmur of customers chatting. I notice Christine waving to me from the corner. I wave back and order myself a herbal tea and come to join her.

Christine sits holding her coffee cup and starts to tell me about her father caring for her mother for many years. She describes how her mother is now very disabled and hoisted in and out of bed. Christine relays to me all that her father has said, including that he feels he is purely existing to care for another. I nod and listen. She also tells me about her mother's head hanging onto her chest but not wanting help to support it.

She then shakes her head despairingly, 'But what can I do, Sara? My parents live in another country and I am working here in London, rarely able to see them.'

I gaze back at Christine. 'I can understand how your father feels. He's been caring for a very long time. It can get the best of us. I know. I've been there.'

Christine half smiles as I continue, 'From the sound of it, there are a few things going on here. This scenario is cyclical. Apparently 80% of communication is non-verbal. As your father feeds your mother abruptly, she will certainly notice that he is helping her because he *has* to, not because he *wants* to. He's feeding and taking care of her purely out of obligation.'

Christine slowly nods as I continue, 'The trouble is, your mother will undoubtedly be noticing this, which will make her feel even more of a burden. In turn, your father will sense this, and on top of his frustration at having to care, he may be feeling pangs of guilt, which she may then be picking up too. All these negative emotions will be circling around, not making for a good atmosphere for either of them.'

Christine has pulled a notepad from her handbag, quickly scribbling down my observations. I continue, 'Your mother clearly feels she is a burden but she still deserves quality of life. She must love your coming to visit, and she deserves to be able to see you when you are able to catch up. I think it's time to ensure the headrest is added to her wheelchair, so she doesn't hurt her neck.'

Christine continues to write as I finish with one more thing. 'Will your father listen to you, Christine?'

'Yes, yes. He is desperate to try anything right now.'

'Well then, could you ask him to make an agreement with himself? When he awakes the next morning, can he agree to do *everything* with love, not just for his wife, but also for *himself?*

Not just in feeding and taking care of her, and not just in every small chore he does that day, but in everything he does for *himself*?'

Christine continues to take notes.

'Then, when he goes to bed that night, to ask himself, does he feel *any* better?'

Christine looks up at me smiling and puts down her pen. We finish our cuppas and say our goodbyes.

Although I don't hear from Christine over the next six weeks, I then see her again at another networking group and we happen to meet in the doorway before we both head in. Christine greets me with a huge smile and gives me a hug, 'Sara, thank you so much! *Everything* has changed.'

'That's great!' I exclaim.

'I shared your advice with my father and he took it on board. Then, when I was back visiting them this last weekend, I watched him taking care of Mum. He was completely different. He was very caring and lovingly fed her. Afterwards he actually asked mum if it was okay for him to go for a bike ride. She nodded and said, "Yes, of course". He then headed off for a few hours.'

'That's wonderful, Christine,' I smile.

'Not only that, but the atmosphere in the house has lifted. They have noticed this shift, and are now looking at new ways to improve their lives. For example, previously Dad would physically pick up Mum to transfer her into the car – dangerous for both of them. But now they order a wheelchair taxi to save his back and keep Mum safe.'

'I am so relieved for them,' I tell her.

Christine continues, 'I suggested to Mum that the headrest be added to the wheelchair at all times, but she wants to keep exercising her neck, so instead, she is hoisted into bed a few times a day.

'And finally, before this change, I was calling them every day, worried sick, but now I know they are alright, I call them just once a week for a catch up. I can now get on with *my* life, here in London.'

I give Christine another big hug after hearing her wonderful news and we head into the event.

In her parents making just a few simple changes to their daily routine, not only had it improved the quality of life for them, but for their daughter as well, causing a ripple effect.

Creating your own positive shift

Are there any small changes you can make to your life to make it easier? If you become stressed in thinking about having to do something, stop for a moment and ask yourself: 'Why?' Do you really have to do this thing, or is there anything you could do differently to help your situation? Also, if you are constantly stressed or low, others around you may be picking up on this. We can affect each other without realising it, making it all the more important to look after yourself and ensure your own happiness.

> *The smallest changes to daily life can make the biggest differences*

As well as giving love to the person you care for, can you also give *yourself* that same degree of love? You will not only feel better, but be more equipped to be there for your loved one. Each day will be easier to bear and more enjoyable too.

Over to you…

- Try surveying your entire day and see where changes could be made, however small, to improve your and your loved one's lives?

- Are there any chores you loathe doing? You could try doing them with love and see if it makes you feel better. Or else, try listening to some uplifting music, or a podcast, whilst doing something you don't particularly enjoy, to take your mind off the chore?

- Even though the smallest changes can make the biggest differences, try not to make too many changes in one go. Your loved one may not appreciate too much change. If something does not work, don't give up but try another way.

26

You are so much more

Many long-term carers are defined by their caring role. Their identity has disappeared as they tell anyone they greet that, first and foremost, they are a carer. It may even be the first thing they mention. Caring has become the dominant factor.

I certainly noticed my identity reduce whilst caring. One time whilst on holiday and on a boat trip out at sea, I started chatting with a woman in her 30s, with her young son sitting beside me. She asked me what I did for a living. Of course, it didn't take long before I started to recount my tale of woe. As I shared my life of marriage to a man with brain cancer, she started to cry. I took a sharp intake of breath.

'Oh my God!' I thought. 'What is *wrong* with me? I have come away to have a break, but not only have I been focusing on illness and caring, I have actually upset someone else on *their* holiday.'

Well, she did ask. But even away from my caring duties, I still had them clearly etched in my mind. That would never make for a good break. Furthermore, I was not making the most of my holiday. So, from that point forward, I decided to make a concerted effort to enjoy myself and not dwell on the difficulties back at home.

It is not good to become totally absorbed by our caring role, especially when we want to have quality time when having a break. Also, we don't want to drain ourselves and those around us with our continuing care challenges. There are still other things to focus on and enjoy.

Try not to let caring take over your whole existence

Don't get lost in your roles

Many carers experience 'role confusion'. Being thrust into the responsibility of caring can make it difficult to separate out our other roles, including being a partner, mother, father, son or daughter. You have many roles besides being a carer. For example, I was not only a carer, but a wife, daughter, designer, musician, gardener, cleaner, physio, Nurse Ratched and more! At present, you may be caring, but this is not all you will be doing during your lifetime.

At times I felt I was Neal's mum more than his wife. That was when I realised I needed to step back a bit from caring and return to being more of his wife again.

Caring, but not the carer

I heard a motivational speaker discuss the role of caring. She came out with a great phrase that struck a chord with me: 'Caring, but not the carer'.

Caring was to be viewed as something that I was *doing*, rather than something to be defined by. Even if we play a particular role for quite some time, it doesn't mean that is all we are and always will be.

Your present situation as a carer should not imply you are solely here in the world to look after another. You are so much more. You are also here for yourself – to experience and enjoy life.

Daniella's story

One afternoon, I meet Daniella for a coffee and a catch-up. For years she cared for her mother, who has recently died. As I greet Daniella and give her a hug, she proceeds to tell me all about the events leading up to her mother's death.

Daniella is a little older than me, but certainly not that old. Even so, her hair is grey, long and straggly and she has a sallow complexion. She is also thin and definitely looks older than her years. I wonder how she looked before she began caring for her mum. Have the years of caring aged her?

Now her mother has gone she is trying to decide what to do next. She has a few friends nearby and she has been working part-time whilst caring. Now, short of money and on her own, she is looking to sell up and move away. As she shares her plans with me, I can't help thinking that, after all her selfless years of caring for her mother, she seems to have very little to show for it. It is all rather depressing. She has given so much of her self to caring, and now her mother has gone, her life appears to be empty. Bereaved and feeling quite alone in the world, her new challenge is to rebuild her life again. I really feel for her.

As I come away from our catch-up, I suddenly have alarm bells ringing in my ears: 'Don't you *ever* find yourself in that position,' I tell myself.

Invest in yourself

As busy as we are with caring and other commitments, we still need to invest in ourselves. Even though you may see your social life suffer, try to continue nurturing friendships. We all have good friends we have known for years, and we still want those friends in our lives for years to come. This may mean making an effort to call them, even if they haven't called you. You could even text to touch base. It doesn't take much to connect and it can really make a difference to the quality of your life. If you can manage to find a way to keep some of your own life intact, this will bode well for your future.

Keeping the grey matter going

Peter's father had cared for his mother for many years after she had a stroke. As his father was stuck at home caring all day, he kept his mind occupied by teaching himself Spanish and Italian, using language CDs. I thought this was a great idea. Not only would this have helped keep his mind sharp, but it would also have given him something to focus on, whilst caring for his wife. Learning something new and being able to speak two foreign languages would have given him a sense of achievement.

Your caring role may become redundant one day, but your life will continue. Putting effort into investing in yourself on a regular basis will help to enrich your present and future.

Over to you...

- Have you allowed your caring role to define you? Have your other roles become blurred? You are so much more than 'a carer'. What other roles do you have?

- When you see friends and family, how often do you allow the topic of illness and caring to dominate the conversation? Why not set a time limit on how long you discuss your caring role and the issues arising from it? You can then look at fun things to talk about. You could even talk about old times, which can lead on to other subjects.

- What do you enjoy that keeps your mind occupied? Is

there anything else you would like to learn? It doesn't need to be as challenging as learning a new language. There are easier leisure pursuits that can be very rewarding. For example:

o   You could try watching online documentaries. There are free programmes on TV channels and YouTube.

o   Is there anything you would like to know more about? You could read up on a particular subject and look online to find out more. Neal loved Egyptology. After he was diagnosed and unable to work, he enrolled in a course for two hours a week. Not only did this class break up his week, he made new friends. At the end of term, I would drive him to the Natural History Museum to meet his class for a tour, so I also ended up benefiting. Also, there are many online courses, so you wouldn't have to leave the house if this is an issue for you.

o   If you have outside space, why not try your hand at gardening? When I first moved in with Neal, I had no idea about gardening, but over the years I have learnt on the go. By keeping the garden looking good, with beautiful flowers, and seeds out for the birds, it is my little bit of paradise to relax in on a summer's day.

o   I bought an iPad for Neal, when he became too disabled for board games. I downloaded free or cheap Apps for him to play. Some were musical, such as a piano keyboard to play on, whilst others were visually stimulating, which was good for someone with a neurological disorder. Others exercised his eye-hand coordination. On Neal's iPad, I also added a music playlist, with songs he loved to listen to whilst he lay in bed.

o If you feel too tired to read, why not listen to audio books? There are many available. I used to listen to audio CDs with Neal and we became lost in gripping tales.

o There are many great podcast series to listen to, of all genres – including comedy, health and sport. Try searching the internet for 'Podcast' and see the choices available. Most are free and you can listen to them on your computer or smart phone.

o You could discover new music. Try online music websites or music services like Spotify. Music can soothe the soul and you can become absorbed in a track.

o There are many arts and crafts you could try, including knitting or crochet.

o Do you enjoy cooking? Not only can cooking be therapeutic, but you benefit at the end. There are many easy and inexpensive recipes online.

o Take up Tai chi, yoga or other relaxation classes. I took up a yoga class to stretch and strengthen my back. I then continued the exercises at home.

o Go to free community events. Charities and your local organisations will hold free or low-cost events throughout the year. Check them out on your community homepage or in your local newspaper.

27

The 'D' word

If you are caring for someone with a serious medical condition, or who is elderly and infirm, you will be aware that you may have limited time with them – something most carers are acutely aware of. This is why caring can be so painful. You have to be a pillar of strength for them, whilst deep down knowing they could soon be gone.

In wanting to be strong for our loved ones, we can often bottle up our emotions, because we don't want them to worry about how *we* are feeling. They are dealing with their own issues.

If you feel your emotions become overbearing, try confiding in friends and family who will be understanding. In addition, you could ask your doctor or charities whether you can receive counselling. I had counselling sessions at my local carers' centre. Before I went I didn't believe they would do much for me. I was supposed to agree to six sessions, but I thought I'd try just the one and decide after that. I'm so glad I went. The counsellor was a great listener and asked me the right questions, which brought up emotions I didn't want to confront. I would often say to her, 'Oh, do I really have to think about *that*?' and laugh.

The counsellor would reply, '*That's* why it would be good to talk about it.'

Her questions helped me uncover deep-rooted emotions,

some of which I had suppressed for years. Afterwards, I would go for a walk to digest all that we had discussed. Opening up to a stranger, such as a counsellor, can help us air our thoughts and feelings and bring us to a better understanding of what is happening around us and to us. There are also counselling sessions that can be taken over the phone, if you would rather not speak to someone face-to-face. You can search the internet to find out more.

If you are caring for someone with limited time, the grieving process may start well before they have actually gone. Also, you may need to have important conversations with them before they pass. These can be very emotional times.

Deciding a fitting tribute

There was one other thing I really wanted to get clear on before Neal deteriorated any further, and that was the arrangements for his funeral. It's an awful question to ask someone you love. I remember years before, Neal commenting to my mum, as they sat in the living room, that when he was gone, he wanted his ashes to be scattered on Somerset Cricket Ground. As I overheard this while making tea for them in the kitchen, I called out, 'You're not going to be scattered anywhere, Neal, because you're not going anywhere!'

Though, in saying that, I was glad he had made this part clear, if and when the time came. I knew I needed to discuss with Neal his funeral arrangements in a sensitive way; then, one day, I had an idea. After I had been at a meditation class at our carers' centre, I sat with Neal on the sofa with a cuppa, telling him about the relaxing music in class that morning. I told him that we had then discussed the music we would like played at our funerals. I said for mine, I would like *Time of Your Life* by Green Day and asked him what he would choose. Over the next few minutes, I listened intently. Neal supported Saints, Southampton Football Club, so he said he would like *When The Saints Go Marching In* – apt for a funeral. He also said how he would like to have his funeral down near his family and where most of his friends lived. Finally, he told me he wanted both myself, and his best friend to speak and give eulogies. *That* I was not expecting. But I was relieved to know what he wanted and not to have to bring it up in conversation again.

Nobody likes to talk about funerals, but every now and again the topic will arise – they are part of life. Tara and Daniel were good friends we had met at the hospital, as Daniel had also been diagnosed with a brain tumour. We loved meeting them for lunch now and then. I knew Daniel had worsened and, one morning, Tara rang to tell me he had died. It was very sad news, especially as, like Neal, Daniel had only been in his 40s.

'Will you and Neal come to the funeral?' Tara asked.

I knew Neal might be sensitive about Daniel's passing and funeral, especially as they suffered from the same condition. Daniel's time had come and Neal would undoubtedly wonder when his would be.

'I would love to be there, Tara,' I said, 'but I'm not sure how Neal will take it. I'll let you know.'

Later, I walked into the living room and told Neal the depressing news. I sat on the sofa opposite and I asked him if he would like to go to Daniel's funeral. His answer surprised me: 'Why would I want to go to the funeral of someone I hardly know?'

Neal knew Daniel quite well, but I realised that this news was too awful for him to take in.

'Well, have a think about it and let me know if you change your mind,' I replied.

A few days later, Neal asked me, 'What day is the funeral?'

I smiled. 'It's next Thursday.'

'I think I'd like to go,' he replied.

I walked towards the phone. 'I'll let Tara know we're coming.'

Neal had needed to process what had happened to his friend. The following week we headed to Daniel's funeral and caught up with Tara. It was good to show our support.

A few years later, another of our friends, Sean, who had also been diagnosed with a brain tumour, went into palliative care and we knew he might not have long to live. Neal was an atheist and believed that when you died, that was it. There was no more. So a question he asked one day surprised me. He asked, 'Can I pray for Sean?'

I sat beside Neal and said, 'Of course.'

We can pray anywhere at any time. We don't have to be in church to pray. And so he did. I personally believe the same applies to funerals. If we find them overwhelming, especially if we are having a difficult time with our own illness, I don't believe we have to go. Instead of attending, we could do something else to remember the loved one, like going for a walk or sitting in a beautiful garden to think about them and send our love. But if we can, it's good to attend the funeral of a loved one, to show our respect and also support those left behind.

When Neal finally passed, one of our good friends, Jackie, declined from attending his funeral. Jackie's son was Sean, who had sadly passed away a few years before, and the thought of attending Neal's funeral was something she couldn't bear. I couldn't blame her. It was her choice and I knew she had been feeling very low. Instead, she sent a card and her love.

A very low ebb

If your loved one's condition is worsening, their mental state may also be deteriorating.

After Neal's stroke, he was practically a body in a bed. He

couldn't do anything for himself and could only say a few words once in a while. Being unable to express his feelings must have been horrendously frustrating. One afternoon, as I perched on his bed, spoon-feeding him chocolate mousse, he spoke two words to me very clearly.

'Commit suicide.'

I was shocked and paused in feeding him. Neal was always an optimist, and even after diagnosis, he had said how much he loved life, but the years of illness and disability had finally taken their toll. It was a surreal moment. I stared into Neal's eyes as he gazed back at me. I wasn't sure what to think or say. I knew Neal was depressed. He was on antidepressants to treat his brain tumour. Those two words frightened me and I slowly resumed feeding him in silence.

When I went back to the kitchen, unnerved by his words, I thought about what I could do. I felt I knew that if I said the word 'Dignitas' to Neal, he would probably put his thumb up – his only way of communicating. Dignitas is a society based in Switzerland that provides assisted suicide to those with a terminal illness, either physical or mental.

As much as I wanted Neal's suffering to end, I couldn't face taking him there. Also, I didn't want Dignitas to be the end of our story – I loved him too much. Not only this, but I would have been criminally responsible for his death and imprisoned, as assisted suicide is against the law in the UK. Furthermore, I'm not sure what his family would have made of it either. But it was about Neal and *his* life, it was not about me, or his family.

Later, I told Neal I loved him so very much, but I didn't talk about ending his life. Looking back now, I wish I had, although he wouldn't have been able to express his thoughts and feelings. Instead, I hugged him and told him I knew life was grim, and I would do my best to make the most of every day with him.

I know this makes for depressing reading, but it's good to be aware, in case your loved one becomes very low. If their condition involves mental illness, they may have already talked about ending their life. During this difficult time, all we can give is our love and support.

We don't want them to go, but we don't want them to suffer

If you, or your cared-for, do experience any suicidal thoughts, please, please, do not keep them to yourself. Speak to your doctor or a healthcare professional you know and trust. Please don't allow these feelings to go unchecked. You are so loved. Suppressed emotions can cause further mental and physical problems for both of you. As the saying goes, 'Better out than in'. Share your inner thoughts and feelings with others to help improve your mental health.

One day during Neal's last summer, he headed off to the hospice day centre for his weekly visit. Whilst he was out, I decided to go for lunch with a good friend. We sat outside, enjoying a glass of wine in the sunshine. As we chatted, I received a call from the hospice on my mobile. This surprised me and instantly had me worried for Neal. The nurse asked: 'Hi, Sara. Have you noticed how much worse Neal is?'

I racked my brain. He hadn't looked any different to me that morning.

'Well, he's been *bad* for years,' I replied. 'That's how he always is.'

'I'm sending him home this afternoon with morphine, just in case,' she told me.

I didn't like the words 'morphine', or 'just in case'.

Seeing Neal every day, I hadn't noticed that he had declined further. It had been too subtle day-by-day for me to pick up.

When Neal arrived back home, I was more alert to see what she had meant. I respected a hospice nurse's years of experience and I dwelt on the fact that Neal's time might be drawing to a close.

Over the next few weeks, Neal remained the same, but I didn't. I became low, as I knew he was reaching the end. Whilst I struggled with this thought, Neal perked up again and became clearly better. I was relieved, and felt better myself, but I knew we might not have long. It was during this time that I decided to write Neal's eulogy – the words I would say at his funeral. Because I knew how dreadful I had been feeling as Neal had worsened and I realised I would probably feel equally low when he finally passed, I probably wouldn't then be in the right frame of mind to write a fitting tribute to my husband.

So I sat down to write Neal's funeral speech. I wanted a lot of his humour in it, as he was so funny and cheeky. I needed words to celebrate his life. He was such a great guy with a huge heart, and I wanted his eulogy to capture this. The following true story appeared in his eulogy, and gives you an idea of Neal's humour. I can only apologise!

One day, arriving at hospital, Neal and I were with his oncologist to receive his MRI scan results. Neal's specialist was a lady in her late 40s, very tall, very thin and very posh. She wore tweed A-line skirts and had a bob of short brown hair. As we entered her consulting room together and sat down, Neal immediately spoke: 'Doctor, are my testicles black?'

Both the oncologist and I looked up abruptly and stared at Neal. He repeated his question, 'Doctor, are my test results back?'

The oncologist gave Neal a wry smile. Only Neal could have got away with that.

*Another joke I would often hear him say was, 'When
I go, I want to go peacefully in my sleep, like my father.'*
*Neal's dad had died years before and had worked on
the trains. So we would all nod with Neal in agreement,
but then he would add, 'Not like his passengers,
screaming.'*
He was a cheeky one.

When autumn came, Neal's health had deteriorated further.
He looked depressed and the days were grim. I felt he was
holding onto life, not just for himself but for me as well. As I
have said, Neal was not religious and believed that, when you
are gone, you're gone. He was probably, and unsurprisingly,
afraid of dying.

At the time, I had read a wonderful book called *Dying To Be
Me: My Journey from Cancer, to Near Death, to True Healing* by
an Indian author, Anita Moorjani. Anita writes of growing up in
Hong Kong and never feeling that she fitted in. She desperately
tried to please others and, in turn, lived a fearful life. Sadly, she
became ill with cancer which ravaged her body for years. She
became emaciated and finally fell into a coma, breathing what
was thought to be her last, in an intensive care ward in hospital.

As doctors and nurses attempted to keep her alive,
unbeknown to them she had left her body and was looking
down upon herself, lying in the hospital bed. All her pain
and suffering had gone. Instead, she felt only immense and
unconditional love around her and the spirits of her father and
best friend, both of whom had died years before, were with her.
They told her it wasn't her time yet.

Anita had endured years of suffering cancer and was not up
to going back and living as she had. Although she could have
gone on to death, in that moment she understood that it was
fear that had left her so physically unwell. She agreed to go back

into her body, relieving her family, who had been expecting the worst. She now understood more about life and how she wanted to really live, and, in doing so, she amazingly recovered within weeks. This was all documented by the hospital.

I loved Anita's account of her 'near-death experience' (NDE) and what it meant for us all. We are so much more than our bodies, and death is not final. So I decided to read the inspiring chapter about her NDE to Neal one evening as he lay in bed. He listened attentively as I read her words, and, when I finished, I turned to him and said, 'So you see, Neal, you shouldn't be afraid to die. We *all* have to go, but it's only our body that dies. *You* don't actually die. When you go, you will feel all this unconditional love and wonder why you hadn't left sooner.'

I looked into his eyes and asked, 'Did you enjoy that?' In a split second, he raised his thumb up to commuicate that he had.

A week later he was gone. I felt that reading this passage had given him permission to go.

His funeral was a celebration of life

Neal's funeral took place just over a week afterwards. Knowing the kind of guy he had been, I wanted to make his funeral a celebration of life. There had been enough suffering for us all during his illness. His favourite colour was royal blue and I asked everyone, if they had anything blue, to wear it on the day. It was wonderful to see so many of Neal's friends and family together, some of whom had flown over especially to the UK. Never again would all these people congregate in one place.

As we entered the crematorium, a trumpeter played *When the Saints Go Marching In*, as he'd wanted. Three of us spoke and, at times, the whole congregation were in stitches as we shared Neal's funny stories. I finished my eulogy by saying how proud I was of him for being so brave, for so many years.

As funerals go, it was a good one, with many happy memories shared.

Afterwards, at the reception, we put large boards up around the room with photographs of Neal from over the years. They were all taken in happier times. I refused to have any of Neal in his wheelchair. I knew he would have wanted to be remembered as the big man he was – confident, kind, and with a great sense of fun. The day was a great send off for a very special man.

Over to you...

- Have you been offered counselling whilst caring? We have so much to deal with, including fearing the loss of a loved one. You can ask your doctor or local charity to see if free counselling courses are available. If offered, you could try just one session to see if it helps.

- If you believe your loved one may only have limited time left, have you been able to chat to them about their funeral arrangements? This can be an awkward conversation and not everyone will be best pleased when asked. You could try sharing with them the music you would have at your own funeral, as I did with Neal, and find out whether they have an idea of what they would like at theirs.

28

You are amazing

If you are a carer, you are amazing! Continuing to care for a loved one shows real dedication, strength and resilience. Not everybody can do it. I know of some who have walked away. They could have been there for loved ones in times of their need, but instead they chose to turn away. So, remember, not everyone can do what you do.

Giving up your time, energy and life to be there for another is without doubt an inspiring and selfless act and it's not easy. When other carers share their life stories, I often tell them how humbled I feel. Although they often say they don't feel like they are doing anything particularly special, they are, and so are you.

One man, who cared for his wife for over a decade, told me that, what had surprised him the most had been his capacity for love. He said, 'Many of us do not have the opportunity to demonstrate the expanse of love for a spouse that caring offers. Actions always speak louder than words.'

He discovered that people around him were genuinely inspired by the way he cared for his wife. He had not expected to be an inspiration, especially whilst caring. He felt that the many years of looking after his wife had defined him as a human being. Caring had given him purpose and integrity. It had made him feel a fuller and more rounded person. He discovered that caring was a vehicle for positive influence in the world. In times of challenge, we discover our worth and what we are capable of.

A few years ago, I heard a neurosurgeon speak to Parliament. We were there to help raise awareness and funding for Brain Tumour Research. During his speech, he said he was often asked what the best criteria were for surviving a brain tumour. Naturally, those listening, including myself, assumed his answer would involve the latest treatments and medicines available at the time, but his answer surprised us all. He said that the best criterion for survival was marital status.

I loved his insight. I personally believe that you don't actually have to be married, but if the person diagnosed has someone there for them, loving them and fighting their corner, this gives them both physical and emotional support. Not only this, but they have a reason to live – the love of another – you!

If you are caring for a loved one, you are not just giving them a better quality of life; you may also be extending their years as well. Your love and support can give another a better chance of survival.

No act of kindness is ever wasted

During my 13 years of caring for Neal, I felt our love deepen. It felt immense and I had never felt love like it before. During those years, not only did I experience unconditional love for Neal, but caring transformed me in a number of ways. I remember how impatient and frustrated I became when I started to care for him, but, by the end, I had changed for the better. I am now so much calmer and more understanding.

Challenges help us to grow, and out of the pain can come intense learning about life. Not only is caring a physical challenge, but it can be emotionally painful. We experience situations and conversations that we might have never previously encountered. Relationships with others, along with ourselves, may be put to the test. We often need to adapt and view things differently to how we did before. As hard as it can be, caring can help us to evolve and become more enlightened.

> *'Suffering in life can uncover untold depths of character and unknown strength for service.*
> *People who go through life unscathed by sorrow and untouched by pain tend to be shallow in their perspectives on life. Suffering, on the other hand, tends to plough up the surface of our lives to uncover the depths that provide greater strength of purpose and accomplishment. Only deeply ploughed earth can yield bountiful harvests.'*
>
> Billy Graham

Sadly, not everyone around you will marvel at your selfless and inspired actions. We are often surrounded by people who don't truly understand what we are going through, or what we have given. It is very easy for others not in our position to judge and give opinions from afar. I'm sure we've all been guilty of that at times.

> *'A lion does not look around when a small dog barks.'*
>
> African proverb

Your love and care for another show you are as courageous as a lion. If others who are not in a caring role are judging you, their flippant comments are like the bark of a small dog. You do not need to turn and engage with their negative opinions. Your energy is better spent elsewhere – either on your loved one, or on yourself.

If your efforts are not appreciated by those around you, you can find ways to acknowledge your hard work and reward yourself. You could make a list of the positive outcomes your caring has achieved. When you feel low or that your hard work and efforts are in vain, refer back to this list to reinforce how important a contribution you make every day.

Caring can test the best of us

Looking after another can be difficult for the toughest of us, so do not go beating yourself up. You are doing your best, whilst achieving something remarkable. It is bound to take its toll on you now and then.

Caring for another is an inspiration to others, so recognise all that you do

Life, and its challenges, in particular caring, is a work in progress. There will be days when you feel you have nailed caring and are enjoying life again. Then another day, you will struggle to cope once more. Ensuring you take it easy on yourself, both emotionally and physically, whilst remaining fit and healthy, will stand you in good stead to enjoy your life, even whilst caring.

There is no magic wand – I wish there were. You will not be able to control everything that caring throws at you. Try not to see your caring role as a burden, and still look to enjoy your life. Being there for yourself will help you to be there for your loved ones.

Over to you...

- Whilst caring, have you learnt anything about yourself? Is there anything you have done which you had never done before your caring role? It's amazing what we are able to learn when we are pushed.

- Has anybody paid you any kind compliments about your caring?

- If they have, why not keep a record of them? It's easy to let compliments wash over us, but sometimes, when we are not feeling our best, it's good to remind ourselves of them. Remember you are doing something amazing – caring for a loved one. Just remember to care for you too.

Information for healthcare professionals and those supporting carers

1. Introduction

Two in three of us will be a carer during our lifetime, and as we become an ageing population, many of us will struggle to care. From previous Carers UK surveys, up to 70% of carers fall either mentally or physically unwell, as did I. Personally, I know of a number of carers who have fallen long-term sick themselves almost immediately after the cared-for had died.

One lady I knew, cared for her husband for many years after he was diagnosed with a brain tumour. Only eight weeks after his passing, she was diagnosed with Multiple Sclerosis and was already in a wheelchair. Their son, in his early 20s, was now caring for her, along with grieving for the loss of his father. This ripple effect of illness can mar any family that has a carer, but there *are* ways to stem the suffering, as I have come to research and discover, and which I will share in this chapter.

To add one more statistic, a recent review, funded by the Home Office, found that 1 in 6 domestic homicides involved a carer*, and the majority of the suspects had mental health issues.

The pandemic seems to have made it harder for vulnerable carers and those being cared-for to access outside support and help, for both physical and mental needs and for care support. When support is withdrawn, or difficult to access, risks increase.

* 'Vulnerability Knowledge and Practice Programme (VKPP)', Domestic Homicide Project Spotlight briefing #4: carers, November 2022

229

Within the report, the majority of carers involved were the suspect, but there were also carers who became the victim.

Carers may not recognise their experiences or their actions as abuse, and may not realise they can get support or even know where to go to receive help.

Conversely, some carers are pushed to the brink, with talk of committing suicide.

This is why we need to increase awareness for all concerned – from healthcare professionals, to carers, and to the wider community.

It can take up to two years for someone in a caring role to realise they are a carer

So why do so many carers neglect their own health, even cancelling hospital appointments, or turning down respite when offered?

■ 2. The issue: Carers Response Mode

We predominantly live out our lives within our subconscious, which makes up for the majority of the back end of our brain. Only the small portion at the front – the frontal cortex – manages higher level executive functions of cognitive skills including the capacity to plan, organise, initiate, self-monitor and control one's responses in order to achieve goals.

From an early age, we fully live within the subconscious, in fact, up to seven years of age. This helps us to become a sponge in learning, taking life in and making language easier to pick up, helping us to survive. This is why we can become similar to our parents, as we become *programmed* – taking in their unfiltered good, and bad, habits. Think of a something you may have found difficult to learn in the past, but can now do quickly and easily without much thought. Learning to drive could be one such task.

When we get into a car for our first lesson, there is so much to take in – the gear stick, the mirrors, indicator, break pedal and steering wheel to name but a few. It can feel daunting on that initial session, manoeuvring someone else's car down the road.

Fast forward to present day. Chances are, when you climb into your car to drive somewhere, you've probably been listening to good music, taking in the views and thinking of what else you need to do that day. Driving has become second nature because you have become *programmed* to drive. It is now hardwired into your subconscious, making life easier.

This also applies to caring. At first there is so much to deal with. Caring is complex. I think back to hoisting my 16 stone husband in and out of bed, washing and changing him. At first it was hard. Really hard. He was big and heavy and unable to speak. But years later, I could whizz him back and forth from the wheelchair to the bed at a moment's notice. Even the paid carers, who had come to help, looked surprised when I did this one afternoon as he needed to be in bed swiftly. This was because it had been *programmed* into my subconscious, making my life easier.

Caring is complex

For carers, there are many skills we have to learn quickly, and it will not just be the physical side. There will be emotional and mental elements we have to consider. For example, my husband's mother was elderly. I didn't want to give her an unnecessary sleepless night if I had called an ambulance again to get Neal to hospital. I would inform other members of the family, but give her a shortened version of the news the next day, because I knew she suffered physical symptoms upon worrying.

Even within a few weeks of caring for someone, we can become *programmed* in the subconscious to help make life easier. This may all sound good, but as carers, we have also become *programmed* to focus on everyone else around us, but ourselves.

During the sessions I give to carers, I have noticed time and again, that not only do they not put their *own* oxygen mask on first, rather putting it directly onto the cared-for – because they are now *programmed* to care, they start to look around to see who else needs their help.

I have a good friend who has been caring for 30 years. When I ask her how she is, it doesn't take long for her to revert back to her husband – the cared-for. She then talks of others who are suffering and struggling with life. I then place my hand on her arm and reiterate my question, "But how are you? *How are you?*"

■ The strategy: Gaining clarity

During my sessions for carers, I ask them, "How are you?"

This is the first step to help carers recognise how they are actually feeling, as most have no idea.

How are they feeling **mentally?** We have an estimated 70,000 thoughts a day, and many of these are on a negative loop. What kind of thoughts are they regularly thinking?

Secondly, how are they feeling **emotionally?** As thoughts are the language of the brain, emotions are the language of the body, but most of us ignore or suppress our emotions. But our body is communicating with us all of the time, and it is good to connect with it. Ever heard of the 'gut feeling'?

Finally, how are they feeling **physically?** Because negative thoughts and feelings, if left unchecked, can end up impacting the body, leaving us fatigued, depressed and eventually physically ill.

I ask carers to regularly check in with themselves, as I did with a neighbour who was also a carer. We would meet up on a Sunday evening each week over a cuppa. This meeting doesn't have to take long, but allows carers to regularly gauge how they are, and if they are on the slide to ill health. Also, sharing an issue, can help take the weight off a carer's shoulders, allowing them to open up and be heard.

Another way for a carer to regularly check in with themselves is to **journal**. Just a fancy name for a notepad and pen. This can work very well. By jotting down all the issues that are arising and asking themselves how they are feeling, helps to get negative thought patterns out of their head and onto paper, giving them clarity. They can then ask themselves questions on these issues, such as what *can* you do about it? And even if there is nothing they can physically do, they still have a choice of how they react.

Carers can often think they are coping, when actually they are not

■ 3. The issue: Co-dependency

The carer and cared-for's relationship can be complex. Along with *programming* to systematically take care of the other's needs, carers can become *co-dependents*. Self-sacrificing, carers often have no boundaries, harming themselves *and* the relationship with the cared-for. We might also confuse love with being someone's caretaker. Helping becomes compulsive as the carer feels continually responsible for another. They can also become judgemental, making decisions for the cared-for, further disempowering the person they look after. Often unbeknown by the carer, they then take more control.

■ The strategy: Improving self worth and independence

Carers can slip easily into negative patterns of behaviour, especially if they have been caring full time and for a long period. It can take time for a co-dependent person to change their habits for the better, and may need to try multiple strategies to build their confidence and see their own self-worth.

Encouraging a co-dependent carer to have time away from the cared-for, whether it be a short time in the day, or for longer respite, will help to improve their sense of independence.

Each carer is unique, along with the person they care for, so there may be certain triggers which create co-dependent behaviour. Helping a carer to understand the difference between supporting and co-dependency will help give them greater clarity. *(For more information, see page 87).*

Many carers feel solely responsible for the cared-for, which is a huge burden if caring for many years, and so the carer will need as much support from the community and services as possible.

■ 4. The issue: Suppressed emotions

Unconsciously carers suppress their emotions to deal with the job of caring at hand, otherwise they may feel they would be in further overwhelm. In suppressing emotions, you don't then have to feel the negative emotions, such as sadness or anxiety. Carers can then feel more in control of the situation. Many people have learned to repress their emotions, especially if raised in a dysfunctional family. We can then learn how to communicate and control our emotions as a child.

Ignoring our emotions and soldiering on with caring can cause great strain on the body. Many carers are in the constant 'fight or flight' response, switching on the sympathetic nervous system and wearing out the body. Carers can be so used to feeling stressed or anxious that they become used to it. I describe this as being *comfortably uncomfortable,* and carers are not aware that they are now not living in homeostasis.

■ The strategy: Counselling

Counselling is a great way for carers to get in tune with their feelings in a safe environment. A counselling session may bring up negative emotions, leading the carer to express their stress and even cry. This helps to release suppressed emotions, relieving the carer of emotional pressure.

I also benefitted from a series of sessions whist caring. If carers are not keen to commit to six or 12 sessions, I suggest that they try the first one and see how it goes. Just opening up and sharing their inner thoughts can be the first step to improving a carer's health and wellbeing.

A **Carers Assessment** may also help, allowing the carer to open up and talk about all that is happening in their caring role, and the issues they are experiencing. During my Carers Assessment, I would describe the session as lifting the pressure cooker lid, which did me the world of good. After uncontrollably sobbing for an hour, I left the assessment already knowing what I needed to do to make my quality of life and wellbeing better.

■ 5. The issue: Caregivers Burnout

In the United States, they have a term for someone who is physically, emotionally and mentally exhausted when taking care of someone else. There can be many symptoms *(see page 4),* but carers can reduce their risk of burnout in a number of ways *(see pages 9-15).*

■ The strategy: Respite

One particular way is to ensure the carer does not hit crisis and burnout, is to factor in regular respite. For when we are in the midst of caring, we cannot see the wood for the trees. Carers often think they are coping when in fact their mental and physical health may be on the slide. It isn't until crisis strikes and they are unable to care anymore, do they realise how they have *actually* been feeling. And so, getting into the outside space, helps them deal with the inside space. It is often only then that a carer may finally start to take responsibility for their own health and wellbeing, whilst creating healthy boundaries and pushing back and knowing where to say no.

Respite is vital.
As well as giving carers recuperation,
getting into the outside space, helps
them deal with the inside space.

■ 6. The issue: Anticipatory grief

Most carers experience anticipatory grief, which refers to feelings of grief or loss that they may feel before the loss actually happens. Carers can also feel loss in other ways, including seeing their loved one change mentally or physically, or their personality may change due to an illness or condition.

My husband had previously been full of confidence before his diagnosis. Standing at 6'4", nothing fazed him. Years later, with mobility disabilities and continued decline, he became introverted. He struggled to be out of the house for long, preferring the comfort of his sofa. One other carer described him as 'a broken man', something I found deeply upsetting, and I certainly experienced anticipatory grief during this time.

The carer may also have seen the loss of their career and the life they had before their caring role began.

■ The strategy: Mindfulness and breathing

As well as counselling, which has been previously mentioned, **mindfulness** can be a powerful tool to help a carer from worrying about the future and focus on the present.

This technique involves noticing what is happening around them, without judgement. For example, when taking a walk in the park. Instead of being pent up with thoughts and worries, mindfulness allows the carer to use their five senses – looking at all that is around them, breathing in and smelling the flora, listening to the birds and other sounds, and feeling the warmth of the sunshine or the clothes on their body. This allows the person to really experience everything with their body, helping them to focus on the present and enjoy the moment.

Another technique is box breathing. Breathing in for five seconds, holding for five and then out for five. In focusing on the breath, this helps pull away from any intrusive negative thoughts in that moment. In slowing down the breath, this not only relaxes and calms the carer, who may be in the 'fight or flight' mode, it also switches on the parasympathetic nervous system within the body, allowing the carer to feel safe whilst the body goes into the rest and digestion response, decreasing respiration and heart rate, helping the carer to restore energy and even to think clearly as they become centred.

■ 7. The issue: Sleep depravation

Having recurring problems sleeping is common for carers, and can be an ongoing issue when caring for someone. Occasionally having a disturbed night will affect a carer the following day, but having trouble sleeping for longer than a night or two, will make their caring role even harder.

A carer may find that they are constantly tired, dropping off during the day, having trouble concentrating or making decisions, and could even start feeling depressed. Long-term sleep depravation may also increase a carer's risk of having high blood pressure, diabetes and obesity.

■ The strategy: Sleep planning and tactics

Most of us need a good eight hours of sleep to function properly the next day, but carers may have a broken night sleep due to their caring responsibilities. The cared-for may be getting up in the middle of the night, or, as I did, have a baby monitor on, because my husband often had choking fits.

To improve quality of sleep, carers can put into place a number of strategies, including ensuring:

- the bedroom is comfortable. Having the windows open to allow for fresh air to circulate around the room.

- TVs and computer are left downstairs. Blue light, whilst scrolling on a mobile phone can disrupt sleep, but you can invest in bluelight glasses (not expensive) if you need your phone by your bed and you like to read on it

- the bedroom is dark. Black out curtains or the use of an eye-mask boosts melatonin levels in the brain.

- cutting down on caffeine after 4pm, as this increases adrenaline and could keep the carer awake.

- keeping a notepad by the bed. Jotting down anything that comes up that the carer may need to remember the next day, so they do not lay awake trying to remember.

■ 8. The issue: Financial hardship

As well as the mental and physical stress of caring, in 2022, Carers UK published a report, *'Heading for Crisis: caught between caring and rising costs'*, based on a survey of over 13,000 unpaid carers. Within this report, 1 in 6 unpaid carers were in debt as a result of their caring role and their financial situation. This increased to 2 in 5 (40%) of unpaid carers in receipt of Carer's Allowance – who were more likely to be cutting back on food and heating.

■ The strategy: Benefits

If the carer spends at least 35 hours a week caring for someone with an illness or disability, they may be eligible for extra money called Carer's Allowance, *(£81.90 per week (2024),* and if they don't earn more than £151 per week *(2024).*

Also, the cared-for may be entitled to benefits. To discover the full criteria for Carer's Allowance, and to make a claim, go to www.gov.uk/carers-allowance/how-to-claim, or ask the carer to get in touch with their local carers centre or charity, who may organise the claim for them.

9. Other information: Social prescribing

This approach can help carers to improve their health, wellbeing and social welfare by connecting to their community services, which may be run by the council or a local charity.

A carer can be connected to a *social prescribing link worker,* who can give carer time, focusing on what matters to them. Together the social prescribing link worker and carer can coproduce a simple, personalised care and support plan, and help the carer take better control of their health and wellbeing.

For example, signposting the carer to local support groups and condition-specific charities that also support the carer.

Social prescribing is an all-age, whole population approach that works particularly well for people who:

- have one or more long term conditions
- who need support with low level mental health issues
- who are lonely or isolated
- who have complex social needs that affect their wellbeing.

Most GP surgeries across England can help a carer access a link worker. In some areas, they can also find out about link workers through a local website or at voluntary or community organisations.

10. Registering with charities and online newsletters

Both local and national charities will have monthly newsletters, promoting the many sessions to improve a carer's health and wellbeing, and even finances.

Pointing the carer to charities such as Carers UK, the UK's leading national charity, can help give a carer support on a regular basis, and learn of and join online or in-person coffee mornings, courses and relaxation sessions to help boost their health and wellbeing, whilst feeling connected with peer support within their community.

11. Unpaid carers in the workplace

I have been asked to give more and more sessions for companies who support unpaid carers in the workplace. Many large organisations have a carers hub or network, offering support and advice to those who care. After giving a talk in person, which was also broadcast live across the country for one of the UK's largest supermarket chains, I was told that they had an estimated 20,000 working unpaid carers. It makes sense to support employees in a caring role, which will in turn help retain the company's workforce.

Most carers do not feel valued, seen or heard. They are the unsung heroes, caring for the most vulnerable in society.

12. Outreach for carers

It can take up to two years for someone in a caring role to realise they are a carer, and by then they are usually overwhelmed and exhausted. Even though I had written my book on caring and was vocal in my support for carers, my neighbour, who is a similar age to myself, had cared for his wife for nearly three years, but even so, still never saw himself as a carer.

It can be difficult to get the help and support out to those in a caring role who believe that looking after a spouse or family member in need is just a part of life. Furthermore, I have discovered young carers who look after a parent, may also be difficult to locate, as the parents may not be comfortable in admitting their child is a young carer.

I believe the best place to promote support for carers is the one place we all end up going to when we first fall ill – the doctor's surgery.

13. The true value of carers

Carers in the UK save our economy over £162* Billion pounds a year – the cost of a second NHS. But too many carers end up paying with their own health. Without unpaid carers, our health and social care systems would collapse.

A number of years ago, I heard a neurosurgeon speak to Parliament. We were there to help raise awareness and funding for Brain Tumour Research. During his speech, he said he was often asked what the best criteria were for surviving a brain tumour. Naturally, those listening, including myself, assumed his answer would involve the latest treatments and medicines available at the time, but his answer surprised us all. He said that the best criterion for surviving a brain tumour was marital status.

Carers can often increase the cared-for's longevity

I loved his insight. I personally believe that you don't actually have to be married, but if the person diagnosed has someone there for them, being an emotional and physical rock – this is a huge boost. Not only this, but the cared-for still has a reason to live – the love of another – the carer.

Once in a while, when Neal spent a week in the hospice to give me a break, his health would quickly deteriorate. I remember one nurse calling me just as I had got in the car to go and pick him up. She had called to pre-warn me that he had worsened significantly that week. This had felt like a kick in the gut, but as I sat in front of the steering wheel for those few minutes, I realised his deterioration was only due to him being away from me, and in the hospice.

Within a few days back at home, Neal had clearly improved. Caring for him lengthened his longevity.

14. Educating everyone for best outcomes for carers

As I write this chapter, I have been a member of a Health and Wellbeing Board for a few years now. There are 152 boards across the UK, which were established in accordance with section 194 of the Health and Social Care Act 2012. The boards are a formal committee of the council, with responsibility for encouraging integrated commissioning and service delivery across NHS, public health and local authority services to improve health and wellbeing outcomes for the local community.

The board members include doctors, councillors, management within the NHS and those in the voluntary sector.

I had been invited to be the Carer Representative on the board, reading through the many reports and papers before the quarterly meetings. Although carers are highlighted as being of key importance, I often ask many questions during the Q&As of each report – *What about the carers? What about the carers?*

If there is a paper on those living with long-term health conditions, you can bet the majority of those people will have someone caring for them. So who is supporting the carer, and how are they being supported?

One particular report, on safeguarding the vulnerable within the borough briefly mentioned carers, noting they may be caring for a vulnerable child or adult, but in reality, carers can become just as vulnerable. If the majority of long-term carers fall ill, or even long-term sick, would they not need a section within this report to themselves?

We need to make everyone aware of the work still needing to be done, as two in three of us will become a carer

It is wonderful that the Health and Wellbeing board has asked to have a Carer Representative, and having been on the board for a few years now, I have noticed positive changes. In knowing I will regularly ask questions about carers, those bringing the reports to the table have become aware of my presence, ensuring carers are considered and included within the papers.

We need a Carer Representative on *all* boards, to make everyone aware of the work still needing to be done – especially as two in three of us will be a carer during our lifetime. As the population ages, more of us will be needing care to remain as independent for as long as possible in our own homes – and this will often involve an unpaid carer.

I want to thank you for reading this chapter, to look to better support the millions of carers giving their loved ones a better quality of life. In working and collaborating together, we can help to improve their health and wellbeing, whilst raising the value of care.

To learn more about my talks and sessions for carers, please visit www.whocares4carers.com

Further reading

Anita Moorjani, *Dying To be Me: My Journey from Cancer, to Near Death, to True Healing*, Hay House, 2012
Anita gives weekly video talks, which can be found on YouTube or on her website www.anitamoorjani.com. Her book is available in print, ebook and audio formats.

Dr Wayne Dyer, *Your Erroneous Zones: Escape negative thinking and take control of your life*, Piatkus Books, 2009
Wayne has written many books and you can also watch his videos on YouTube. *Your Erroneous Zones* is available in print, ebook and audio formats.

Don Miguel Ruiz, *The Four Agreements: Practical Guide to Personal Freedom*, Amber-Allen Publishing, 2018 (10th anniversary edition in print, ebook and audio formats).

Useful contacts

Here are the national charities supporting carers in other English-speaking countries. Some condition-specific charities in your local area will also support the carers of the loved one, so it is always worth asking. Please do not hesitate to give either your national or local charities a call to see how they can support you.

UK

Carers Trust	www.carers.org
Carers UK	www.carersuk.org
Carers Week	www.carersweek.org
Age UK	www.ageuk.org.uk
Carers Network	www.carers-network.org.uk
Family Carer Support	www.hft.org.uk

UK condition-specific charities supporting carers

Macmillan Cancer Support	www.macmillan.org.uk
Marie Curie	www.mariecurie.org.uk
Cancer Research UK	www.cancerresearchuk.org
The Brain Tumour Charity	www.thebraintumourcharity.org
Mind	www.mind.org.uk
Alzheimer's Society	www.alzheimers.org.uk
Stroke Association	www.stroke.org.uk

Ireland

Family cares Ireland	www.familycares.ie
Care Alliance Ireland	www.carealliance.ie

United States

Family Caregiver
Alliance   www.caregiver.org
Caregiver Action
Network   www.caregiveraction.org
Caring.com   www.caring.com
Family Caregiving   www.aarp.org/caregiving
National Alliance
for Caregiving   www.caregiving.org
Alzheimer's
Association   alz.org/help-support/caregiving
National Adult Day
Services Association   www.nadsa.org
Caring Bridge   www.caringbridge.org

Canada

Canada Caregiver   www.canadacaregiver.com
Canada Cares   www.canadacares.org
ParkinsonCanada-Atl   www.parkinson.ca
ACNA Canada   www.acnacanada.ca
AGE-WELL NCE Inc.   www.agewell-nce.ca

Australia

Carers Australia   www.carersaustralia.com.au
Mind Australia   www.mindaustralia.org.au
Carers SA   www.carers-sa.asn.au
Dementia Australia   www.dementia.org.au

New Zealand

Carers New Zealand   www.carers.net.nz

Index

Index

SUPPORT FOR CARERS

Easy and Effective online Course for Carers

Enjoy taking this user friendly course at your own speed in the comfort of your home, on your computer, mobile or ipad. Simple to use, we look at the six key areas of your life, with our unique Task Shifter at the end of each session – quick and easy, which carers have loved.

- Discover solutions, strategies and tools to take back control of your caring role
- Simple psychology and research shown to help improve your life
- Empowering you to make positive changes for the better
- Boosts your health and wellbeing, whilst making caring easier.
- Helping you make better decisions – not just for yourself, but also for your loved ones.

Informative and inspiring!
I'm looking forward to the next session.
– Sharon, caring for her son

Go to www.whocares4carers.com and click on Carers Course – It's time to invest in you!